HMO PROPERTY

SUCCESS: THE COURSE

by Nick Fox

ISBN: 978-0-9957831-9-5

First published in England in 2017 by Fox Print Partners

For my family, friends and business partners.
You all inspire me daily. Thank you.
Nick

About the author

Nick Fox is an experienced property developer, mentor, author and speaker with a property portfolio worth in excess of £35 million. What is remarkable is that he built this portfolio in less than a decade!

Most people would probably leave it at that sit back and think what a great retirement they will have to look forward to. Nick has other ideas. He is driven to helping others achieve the same levels of success he has enjoyed as a property developer. This book is designed to help other first time property developers learn from the mistakes and successes he has experienced along the way.

Nick's approach to property investment draws upon the wisdom of the world's most successful investors combined with his own experience as a successful entrepreneur.

His first experience of business came early in life at just eight years old in the school tuck shop. Instead of saving up his pocket money, he decided to invest it and make a profit selling penny sweets for the inflated price of 2p each. This may have been small change and seem like child's play, yet buying something for a low price and selling it for a higher price is one of the basic building blocks of any business and that includes property investment.

The return on investment from those tuck shop sweets was 100% and this was an early indication of an entrepreneurial mind-set, which helped Nick grow a technology business from scratch to a multi-million-pound enterprise. He later went on to apply those same basic principles successfully into property investment.

Nick's involvement in property investment was no accident of fate apart from an early introduction in his childhood. He lived in a static home with his mother and everyone was happy with their lot until it burned down and the family was forced to look for alternative accommodation.

Luckily, the insurance money they received for the damage helped them to buy a house, which was a complete wreck. With a bit of hard work this was soon transformed into saleable property and generated enough profit to move onto the next house and so on.

Nick bought his own first property in 1986, at the age of 18 when many young people are still thinking about which University degree to opt for. The property was purchased with the money he had managed to earn and save from his early entrepreneurial market stall trading.

It wasn't until the mid-2000s that Nick decided to jump into property investment full time and before doing so he read every property book and visited every website he could find to gain insight into the world of property from an investor's point of view. Then he soon got stuck in to developing his own portfolio.

Beyond property, Nick is a keen supporter of various charities and a patron of Peace One Day.

He currently lives in London with his partner Samantha, their two sons Harold and Albert and three wonderful daughters Molly, Lily and Masie.

Introduction to the course

This course has been put together by Nick Fox, who, with more than 500 individual rooms let in the East Midlands, is one of the UK's most experienced HMO portfolio investors. It accompanies his book, 'HMO PROPERTY SUCCESS', and is aimed at specialist property investors who are looking to concentrate on the niche House in Multiple Occupation (HMO) market.

HMOs (shared houses) require different investment strategies and management skills to letting 'standard' buy to let homes.

The financials behind the investment are also different and most local authorities apply tougher safety and management rules to HMOs than they do to other properties.

This course takes you through every step of understanding HMOs as an investment, sourcing, acquiring, letting and then managing them in such a way that you maximise your returns. It also guides you through how to ensure you are compliant with all your legal, financial and tax obligations.

The HMO market is vast and growing. Far from squalid bedsits, modern HMO properties are slick and fashionable homes, let by professional landlords to young professional people or students. This course will teach you how to provide decent homes for multiple tenants while realising high yields and profits for yourself.

Assumptions

√ You are either an existing landlord looking at switching your current buy to let homes to shared houses in order to maximise returns, or you are at the start of your property investment journey and want to become a professional HMO landlord. Either way, HMOs are fairly new to you.

√ You are not a finance or property professional but have a general understanding of how the property market works.

√ You have some experience of running a business.

√ You want expert guidance and access to reliable information, but do not need 'hand holding'

How the course works

Each part of the course contains:

- Detailed information for you to read

- The relevant chapter of Nick's book, 'HMO PROPERTY SUCCESS', which is available from Amazon.co.uk in paperback, Kindle and audio CD versions, and on iBook

Some spreadsheet and document templates to help you. All these templates are available to download as PDFs or spreadsheets from nickfox.co.uk

- A checklist that should be completed and ticked off as you carry out your research and preparation

Although it's intended that you work through the course chronologically, there is no restriction on the order in which you complete the parts.

Course Contents

Disclaimer

This course is not intended to provide personalised legal, financial or investment advice. Readers should seek professional advice with regard to such matters as interpretation of the law, proper accounting procedures, financial planning and tax before proceeding with any property investments. The course author and publisher specifically disclaim any liability, loss or risk which is incurred as a consequence, directly or indirectly, of the use and application of any contents of this work.

Nick Fox's personal disclaimer:

I am not qualified to give financial or legal advice. All related recommendations made in this course should only be considered in consultation with suitably qualified and accredited professionals, particularly as regulations change over time. Persons giving financial advice MUST be properly qualified and regulated by the Financial Services Authority (FSA) and anyone giving you legal advice should be suitably qualified and regulated by The Law Society and the Solicitors Regulation Authority (SRA) (or the Council of Licensed Conveyancers (CLC)).

PART ONE:

UNDERSTANDING YOUR INVESTMENT OBJECTIVES

(Chapter 1 of 'HMO PROPERTY SUCCESS')

This part highlights the key things you need to consider before you embark on your investment journey. It covers goal setting, the personal characteristics and skills of successful investors, looks at why property can be such a good investment vehicle and encourages you to think about whether it's really right for you. Don't be tempted to skip through it, regardless of how prepared you think you already are, as it raises some important issues, and make sure you fully complete the goal setting document and checklist, which will help you focus on what you really want and need from your investment.

Why do you want to invest?

Property as an asset class is generally considered 'a sensible investment choice' for two key reasons:

1. It can provide on going income AND
2. It is highly likely to appreciate in value over time.

By making the right decisions, it's therefore possible for your investment to 'pay your salary' while increasing in capital value to create a pension pot for the future.

But it is impossible to make the right investment decisions unless you have sat down and clearly established the financial and lifestyle motivators behind your desire to invest. Property is only 'a sensible choice' if it delivers on your objectives, suits your attitude to risk and personality, works for your lifestyle and – importantly – you understand that it is a business. Far too many people have ploughed their capital into bricks and mortar with barely a second thought and ended up with something that simply makes their lives a misery.

If you do not go about it in the right way, investing in HMOs can be incredibly challenging, time consuming and labour intensive. The potential financial rewards make it worthwhile, but only if you are able to set up and manage a system to effectively run your portfolio as a real and profitable business.

Particularly in the current economic climate, and at a time when regulation and availability of financing and refinancing is tight, there's a great deal of work to be done before you start looking for property.

If you want to be successful as an HMO investor, you need to start by considering *why* you want to invest.

Your goals

What effect do you want property investment to have on your life? People talk about becoming 'financially free' through property, but the definition of that is different for everyone, depending on their current situation, expectations and desires.

Make a list of exactly what you need and want your investment to give you – financially and in terms of lifestyle – and make each item time specific. The more detailed you can make your goals, the more likely you will be to achieve them.

If you want income, the key questions you need to ask and answer are: how much and by when? Apply SMART analysis to each item on your list, making sure it is:

√ Specific
√ Measurable
√ Attainable
√ Relevant/Rewarding
√ Time bound

For example, in the case of income, you could write: 'In 2 years' time, I am generating £5,000 monthly income from property, enabling me to send my child to private school.'

You must be realistic (you will not make a million in the first 12 months) but, at the same time, don't be afraid to dream big over the longer term. And write each of your goals as though it has already been achieved – don't allow for the possibility of failure. As you make your list, bear in mind that people always achieve their goals more quickly if they are motivated by emotion, rather than purely by money, so attach some kind of personal element to each one.

This is about you, nobody else, so write down everything that is important to you, no matter how trivial you think it might sound to others, for example:

In 6 months' time... I spend the whole of every Sunday with my family I have a massage once a week
My wife has the 4x4 she wants

You can then work out the income and time freedom you'll need to generate in order to realise those goals.

Once you know where you want/need to be in the next 6 months, year, 3 and 5 years, you can start to break that down into shorter periods of time and set the weekly (or even daily) targets you need to hit in order to stay on track to achieve your goals.

GOAL SETTING WORKSHEET

Financial goals overview

How much do you want/need, when and why? Think about both income and lump sums.

Lifestyle goals overview

What kind of life do you want your wealth to allow you to live? What kind of things do you want you, your family and friends to be able to do?

Goals timescale breakdown

Where are you with your investment portfolio, income, pension planning and lifestyle at these key points in time from now? Write in the present tense, as though you have already achieved your goals. E.g. 'I am managing my first HMO and negotiating on the purchase of my second. The additional income has allowed us to upgrade my wife's car to a Honda CRV'.

In 6 months' time, what have you achieved?

In 12 months' time?

In 3 years' time?

In 5 years' time?

In 10 years' time?

Breaking your goals down further...

Now break your goals down into tasks that you can measure on a daily/weekly/monthly basis – whatever feels helpful and achievable for you.

Here is a suggestion for how you could set up a spreadsheet template for annual goal setting, broken down as far as weekly goals:

Goals - <year>		
This year....	Outline of overall goals for the year. 'By the end of the year I am / have....'	

Focus your thoughts on the positives and your time and energy on the things that are within your control

January	Overall goals for month	Week 1: Key goals for this week....	
		Week 2:	
		Week 3:	
		Week 4:	
February		Week 1:	
		Week 2:	
		Week 3	
		Week 4	
March		Week 1:	
		Week 2	Overall goals for quarter
		Week 3	
		Week 4	

<...and so on for the rest of the year.....>

In a year's time...	Summary of where you (and your family) are, financially and personally.
In 3 years' time....	Summary of where you (and your family) are, financially and personally.
In 5 years' time....	Summary of where you (and your family) are, financially and personally.

If you have never set goals before or are not used to working to precise short term targets, I would recommend you read one or more of the books out there specifically about the subject. **Brian Mayne's 'Goal Mapping: How To Turn Your Dreams Into Realities'** is one of the market leaders that I have used myself.

Visual stimuli are very powerful, so make a 'vision board' that illustrates your goals. The more you look at images of what you're aiming for, the more focused and motivated you will be. It can be one sheet of A4 or a whole wall in your office, just make sure it is somewhere you can't miss it

Why property?

As well as providing income and a pension pot, many professional investors choose property because it suits their lifestyle, work ethic, skills, risk profile, personality, tax situation and inheritance plans. These are all things you need to consider carefully.

People who invest seriously in property do so because they believe it offers the most reliable, tangible, flexible, profitable form of investment open to them. That can be broken down into six key aspects:

1. Leverage

No other asset class offers the opportunity to leverage in the way that property does. Banks and building societies lend against property at the level they do because property is seen as having a fundamental 'bricks & mortar' value. Markets peek and trough but a property will almost always hold a certain level of value, so while maximum Loan to Value rates may fluctuate (in the past 8 years, I've seen them fall from 125% to 60% and go back to 85%), you can still leverage other people's money to make a better return on capital than you might otherwise, i.e. you can make your money go further. For example, if there was a 15% rise across all markets:

£100k invested in stocks = £15k growth
£100k invested in £25k deposits on 4 properties, each worth £100k = £60k growth

2. Refinancing

The ability to refinance a property, as an extension to leverage, means you can end up with an income producing asset that has none of your own capital tied up in it. You can't achieve this as quickly and easily as you once could, but if you manage to buy a property at a good price and that particular sector of the market rises sufficiently, you should be able to remortgage in time and release the money you originally invested. By reinvesting that money in another income producing property, you're expanding your portfolio and maximising the return on your capital.

3. Income

With all other asset classes, you mainly profit from growth on the capital. Although there may be interest payments on other types of investment, I haven't found any that offer the same income potential as property.

4. Control

Unlike most other forms of investment, such as stocks or bonds, you have a high degree of control over the investment returns a property provides. While you can't control either the property market as a whole or mortgage rates, you do have the power to decide:

- The type of property you buy
- What mortgage product you have
- How you let the property
- The type of tenants you accept
- The rent you charge (to a certain extent)
- How much you spend on managing and maintaining the property

Essentially, you have a high degree of control over income and expenditure, and, therefore, profitability.

5. Opportunity

The diversity of opportunity to make money from property is really exciting to me, and is one of the reasons it's used by so many people as a wealth creation tool. Whether you want on going income, short/medium term gain, a pension plan, a home for your children in years to come or a lump sum return in the future, property can work for you. You can buy to let single or multiple occupancy units; renovate a property and then sell or remortgage; self build or develop yourself; strike a deal to sell property or land to a developer; get paid for sourcing property; do everything yourself and make it your career, or work with other people to make it a more passive investment... It really does offer a huge variety of options – even one property can allow you to realise different returns at different times in your life, depending on what you need and when.

6. Systemisation

This is a big part of why property works as an investment vehicle for me. If you can put the right systems and team in place to effectively source, acquire, refurbish, let and manage a portfolio, you can reap considerable financial rewards for relatively little of your own time. That frees you up to either focus on high value aspects of your business, or simply to enjoy some of your lifestyle activities. I said earlier that property is a business, and you need to have the ability to establish and manage a 'head office' in a way that works for you. But as long as you can do that, your systemised business should be able to function as a money earner, whether you're there or not.

I have over 20 people working for me, including a PA, a bookkeeper, a property manager, two lettings negotiators and a maintenance team of more than ten contractors. They take care of my income generating portfolio, while I spend my time looking for new HMO deals and work on other property related opportunities. It's good systemisation that's accelerated the growth of my property business and allowed me to pursue other interests – lifestyle and business - in a way that would otherwise be impossible.

Because everyone's situation is different, it is impossible to break down here the pros and cons of property for every possible circumstance. You need to find financial and legal professionals who can advise you properly, both now and into the future, and create an effective advisory and service team around you.

It's particularly important to speak to a wealth advisor. They can look at all your financial interests and plans for the future and help you decide the best way to invest in property to suit your own, personal situation – and whether property is even the right investment vehicle for you.

Chapter 6 of 'HMO PROPERTY SUCCESS': Your team

Once you've researched your local HMO market thoroughly, you should have a level of expertise that very few other people will have. Most of the professionals you'll deal with as you source, buy, refurbish, let and manage your portfolio won't know as much as you do about the market as a whole – and that puts you in a great position for being able to ask the right questions and pick the best people to work with.

There are some very good reasons why you should surround yourself with advisors, suppliers and associates:

1. You can't be an expert in everything, so the very best thing you can do for your business is tap into the knowledge, skills and resources of the people who *are* experts in their own specific area of property investment.

2. By outsourcing as much as possible, you're freeing up your own time. And, as you become better at finding and negotiating great deals and running your business, your time will be worth many times more than the cost of paying someone else to do various jobs.

3. Property can be a lonely business if you do most of the work yourself. You'll find it much more enjoyable with a good team and network around you.

I use the services of more than 20 different people on a regular basis. They are all very good at what they do, which enables me to acquire properties efficiently and for the business to run with minimal daily input from me. I think of these people as my 'team':

- Wealth Manager
- Buy to let specialist property lawyers
- Independent Mortgage Broker
- Accountant
- Bookkeeper
- Estate Agents
- PA
- Property Manager
- Lettings Negotiators
- Project Manager for refurbishments
- Maintenance team and specialist contractors

Since I began investing, there have been some changes to my team, and you may find you don't get the perfect people first time around. But I've worked with all my current advisors, suppliers and employees for a number of years now and am happy that it's a very strong line up.

Your key players

**All professionals giving you financial advice MUST be properly qualified and regulated by the Financial Services Authority (FSA) and anyone giving you legal advice should be suitably qualified and regulated by The Law Society and the Solicitors Regulation Authority (SRA) (or the Council for Licensed Conveyancers (CLC)).*

Wealth Manager

As I've already said, property investment needs to fit properly alongside your other financial interests. Whether you choose to engage a wealth management firm or take advantage of your bank's wealth management service, try to work with someone who either invests in property themselves or already has a number of property investor clients. It'll short cut your discussions and they're likely to have researched the subject very well indeed.

Take your investment objectives and personal financial statement along to your meeting, so that the wealth manager can get a clear picture of your current situation and where you want to get to. They can then help you decide the best way to structure your investments.

Importantly, they can also help you with inheritance planning. Too many people invest in property so they have something to leave to their children, without realising that it can be one of the least tax efficient ways to pass on money. You'll need to amend your Will and may need to set up Trusts – it's a complex area, and demands specialist advice.

As well as being FSA regulated, ideally they will also have the CISI Masters in Wealth Management (MCSI after their name).

Property Tax Specialist / Accountant

Wealth management firms are usually able to give you tax advice and handle your accounts, but you must make sure that you've had a proper discussion with someone who is a property tax expert. As I said earlier in the book, your investment plans will impact your current tax situation, and vice versa, and a specialist will be able to advise you how to set up and run your HMO business in the most tax efficient way.

As well as qualifying under the Association of Chartered Certified Accountants (ACCA), your tax advisor should also be a member of the Chartered Institute of Taxation (CTA).

Mortgage Broker / IFA

Your mortgage broker can make or break a deal. You're looking for someone who understands exactly what you're aiming for and appreciates that things often need to happen quickly. Make sure they're independent (i.e. can access all mortgage products in the market) and have worked in buy to let for a number of years, as they're likely to have established relationships with buy to let and HMO specialist lenders.

I'd never attempt to find a mortgage myself by going direct to different lenders, for three key reasons:

1. It can be incredibly time consuming and I'm not a mortgage expert.
2. Good brokers usually have access to mortgage products that aren't publicised. You only know they're there if you ask about them, and if you don't know they're there…
3. As an individual, trying to contact lenders to progress an application can be an incredibly frustrating experience and you're unlikely to have any luck moving it along quickly. An effective broker will be able to access the right people and push your application through.

Never underestimate the value a good broker can add to your business. Being well financed will mean you'll not only be able to act quickly on deals, but also get better deals and be more profitable.

Any person acting as a broker or making recommendations for your mortgage finance must have one or more of these qualifications/ Certificate in Mortgage Advice (Cert MA) Certificate in Mortgage Advice and Practice (CeMAP) from the ifa School of Finance / Mortgage Advice and Practice Certificate (MAPC) from the CIB in Scotland.

Specialist property lawyer

Ideally, they should be buy to let specialists and have experience of dealing with HMO investors. As with your broker, your legal representative can make the difference between a smooth and speedy transaction and a complete nightmare You can instruct either a solicitor or a licensed conveyancer – both are qualified to handle property transactions – but one of the benefits of engaging a solicitor is that you can choose a firm that also has solicitors specialising in other areas of law. That means your legal representative can tap into the knowledge of colleagues for advice on things like tax planning, Wills, litigation, etc. and you may be able to keep all your legal affairs under one roof.

Some firms have specific case progression departments; some solicitors/conveyancers will progress things themselves. Both have pros and cons - the important things for you to establish are:

1. Are they happy to work to a timescale established at the start (unforeseen circumstances aside)?
2. Will they update you regularly?
3. Will you be able to easily speak to the person directly dealing with your transaction?

You also need to make sure that whoever you choose is happy to liaise and work closely with your broker/IFA and wealth manager to keep your business on track with your objectives.

I realise I'm painting a picture of perfection here, but these legal representatives do exist. Take personal recommendations from other investors and meet in person with all those on your 'shortlist'. Homebuyers usually engage solicitors over the phone or online, but when it's someone who's going to be so crucial to the success of your business over a number of years, you need to make sure there's a good personal relationship and understanding from the start.

The other person who can really help you stay on the right side of the law is a local planning expert. Planning regulations have a tendency to change rather quietly, so if you can build a relationship with a Chartered Town Planner then they can guide you and help you minimize the risk of falling foul of regulations.

Estate Agents
You might be lucky enough to have local estate agents who already understand about investing in HMOs, but it's more likely that you'll have to 'train' them. Avoid agents who want to take your contact details before they've even asked what you're looking for and focus on the ones who actually want to have a conversation with you. You also want someone who knows the area and market well, so try to deal with senior negotiators or the branch manager, as they're more likely to be able to have a productive discussion.

Independent agents are usually owned and/or managed by people who have lived and worked in the area for quite some time. They're often on local boards and well connected, so can be a very useful source of information about planning, upcoming developments, people who might be interested in joint ventures, etc.

Talk to the agents about your plans, show them you have your finances and legal representation in place, then view a few properties and explain exactly what's right and wrong so that they build up a picture of your ideal HMO. Contact and feedback are key; always do what you say you'll do, view properties they recommend right away and keep them posted on what stage you're at in any transactions so they don't need to 'chase' you.

You want to get to a position where you have three or four agents that understand exactly what you're looking for, know you'll act quickly and make sensible offers, so will call you as soon as they see a property that might be suitable. The quicker a sale can be agreed and completed, the sooner the agents get their money – you're an agent's dream – so don't give them any reason not to want to have you at the top of their buyer list.

Agents MUST be members of The Property Ombudsman. Ideally, deal with agents who are Fellows of the National Association of Estate Agents (FNAEA) and/or the Royal Institution of Chartered Surveyors (FRICS)

Reliable contractors
Reliable contractors are worth their weight in gold, and then some. You need a team for your refurbishment projects and then a team that can handle on going maintenance. While you'll probably be able to use many of the same people, some contractors prefer to only handle larger projects and some only smaller ones, which is often the case with electricians and plumbers. The most important thing is that you hire the right people for each job.

Refurbishment core team:
Builder (ideally who can also project manage – otherwise you may need someone else to manage it), preferably a member of the Federation of Master Builders
Plasterer
Painter/decorator
Glazer, FENSA regulated
Locksmith, ideally from the Master Locksmiths Association
Carpet fitter
Plumber, Gas Safe registered
Electrician, 'Part P' registered (check on the Competent Persons Register: competentperson.co.uk)
Cleaner

You may be tempted to project manage the refurbishment yourself, but I'd highly recommend you employ someone else to do it. The refurbishment contractors need to be able to work together; if they all have their own agendas, you can find projects stall or take longer than necessary because they're all blaming each other for not being able to get on to the next stage. A project manager (often a builder) will have a regular team that he knows will work efficiently together and you pay him to make sure everything stays on track. It also means you only have one person to liaise with.

Maintenance core team:
General handyman
Plumber, Gas Safe registered
Electrician, 'Part P' registered (for general maintenance and safety checks)
Portable Appliance Tester
Gardener (the handyman may do this for you)
Emergency locksmith, ideally from the Master Locksmiths Association
Cleaner

You'll need to call on most of these people at short notice, so do everything you can to make sure they respond to you quickly. A very good way of ensuring they do is to make sure you pay them quickly when they invoice. Most – if not all – of these people will be self employed and/or running small businesses and really can't afford to wait several weeks for payment, so will greatly appreciate you settling their bills right away.

"Where do I find good contractors?"

What people are usually asking with that question, is whether I can give them a list of reliable people to use As with so much of this business, you get the best results if you do your own homework, which means networking locally with other landlords and asking friends to recommend contractors they've used. You can also look on websites such as RatedPeople.com and mybuilder.com, where tradespeople have been rated on their work.

Two important things to check are: 1) that any contractor you use has their own insurance and, 2) whether they have some formal accreditation or membership of a relevant industry body, so a good place to start is trustmark.org.uk, which has a database of tradespeople that operate to government endorsed standards. If someone you're considering isn't listed on there, that doesn't mean you shouldn't use them, but do check their credentials thoroughly to make sure they're properly qualified for the job you need them to do, and insured against any damage they might cause.

Gas Safe Register

gassaferegister.co.uk

Federation of
Master Builders
fmb.org.uk

Master Locksmiths
Association
locksmiths.co.uk

FENSA
fensa.co.uk

Trustmark
trustmark.org.uk

The cost of your team

Cost is something that always comes up when I speak to investors who are just starting out and it's a significant concern for those who only have the funds to finance one property initially. They're worried that they're going to end up spending too high a proportion of their money on good advice, particularly with financial and legal professionals, and that's entirely understandable, but legal and financial advice isn't something you should scrimp on.

It's hard to say how much is 'reasonable' for someone to charge you for advice; what I'd say is that you should most definitely feel you're getting value for money. In your initial preparation and research, you should have worked out how much your own time is worth, looked at the risks and associated potential costs of getting things wrong, and therefore be able to work out whether the costs you're being quoted for mitigating those risks and greatly reducing the chance of succumbing to the potential pitfalls of investing are fair.

And when you speak to contractors about what you need them to do, be honest and clear about your future plans. You want to try from the start to use people who will be willing and able to work for you as your portfolio grows.

Building good relationships with all the people on your team is vital to your success. You're going to be dealing with them on a fairly regular basis (some more often than others) so it's important that they're not only very good at what they do and understand your business, but that you actually get on with them.

When you like the people you do business with, and they like you, things get done more efficiently and everyone wins.

"Pretend that every single person you meet has a sign around his or her neck that says 'Make me feel important'. Not only will you succeed in sales, you will succeed in life."

Mary Kay Ash, Entrepreneur

As well as my professional team, I also get a lot of good ideas and advice from other investors and business people that I choose to spend time with. When I started out, I went to every 'property meet' and seminar I could find, but I honestly didn't find them very helpful, mainly because they weren't focused enough on what I wanted to do and there were too many people simply trying to sell to me. That's not to say you might not get something from going along to one or two, but I suggest you be selective.

Visit one or two of the larger national property investment and landlord shows/ exhibitions and listen to as many relevant seminars as you can. If what they say makes sense to you, talk to the speakers afterwards and ask them their opinion on which meets and events are worth attending. And talk to other visitors – you'll find that most people can't wait to discuss their portfolio Make sure you've already done a lot of your objective planning and market research before you go, so you'll really be able to focus on the people you think it might be worth meeting with again.

Is property right for *you*?

Regardless of their personal situation, the one thing all HMO investors need is some significant capital behind them. You should budget at least £50,000 for each property you intend to buy and understand that, unlike pre credit crunch, you're highly unlikely to be able to refinance and release that capital for re investment in the near future.

As well as speaking to wealth and tax specialists to help decide whether property is an appropriate investment vehicle from a financial perspective, there are a number of things you need to consider on a more personal level. Investing in high income generating properties, i.e. HMOs, may suit your financial plans, but…

…are you equipped with the skills to either run an HMO portfolio yourself or effectively manage the outsourcing? Are you:
- Computer & internet savvy?
- A good administrator?
- Organised?
- Motivated?
- Good at time management?
- Able to employ and manage a team of staff?
- Surrounded by a good personal support network?

    …is your attitude to risk in line with the fact that property is considered a medium to high risk investment? Can you accept having millions of pounds of mortgage debt?

    …do you have the people skills to build relationships with other property professionals?

    …do you have the appropriate general business skills to succeed?

    …do you understand financing and how to put together a business plan?

    …will the demands on your time – which are considerable in the first two or three years of building a portfolio – suit your lifestyle?

    …can you project manage? You can outsource renovation and refurbishment management to a certain extent, but you still need to understand all the elements and be able to manage the overall project.

If this is the first time you've run your own business, you must understand and be prepared for the highs and lows you'll experience in the first few years. Read as many books as you can about start up businesses and entrepreneurs - Seth Godin's 'The Dip' is a good one to start with and you'll see that most of them share the same pattern of successes and challenges, and most have failed at some point. To give yourself the best chance of success, I'd recommend that you keep finding out about people who've already succeeded and learn from their mistakes.

I read at least one book a week to help keep my mind and business on track and they are by no means all elated to property. Some of the books that are broadly considered 'personal and professional development' tools are exceptionally good; some are, quite frankly, pretty bad, but there's always something that you can learn from even the poorer ones. You can find a list of the ones that I've found particularly helpful (quite a few of which I've read several times) at the end of this book and on hmopropertysuccess.co.uk.

But I'd say that the best measure of whether you're suited to property investment is the feedback you get from other investors. Spend some time with other people who are already doing what you want to do, talk to them about their property business, see for yourself what's involved in making a success of it and ask yourself whether you can see elements of yourself in them. People have different approaches and not every investor has the same temperament, personal manner, background or goals, but all of them will probably be:

- Self confident
- Committed
- Hard working
- Self motivated
- Self improvers
- People who enjoy business
- Good listeners
- Good negotiators
- Well supported by friends and family

You'll probably have to pay for their time – and almost certainly will in order to access the best – but it will be money well spent, I promise you.

CHECKLIST

Is property investment right for you?

Goals

☐ Listed financial and lifestyle goals

☐ Checked goals have SMART attributes

☐ Made some kind of visual illustration to keep you focused and motivated

Investment options

☐ Put together a personal 'financial statement' (see next page)

☐ Spoken to a Wealth Manager / Financial Advisor

☐ Considered which type of property investment will suit your goals

☐ Identified capital you can access to fund acquisition and refurbishment

Property as a business

☐ Understood the potential risks and rewards

☐ Considered skills required to run a business

☐ Compiled and committed to a reading list

☐ Spent a day with more than one successful investor

Once you've clarified exactly why you want to invest and established that property is the right investment choice to help to realise your goals, you need to look at HMO property investment in more detail.

PERSONAL FINANCIAL SNAPSHOT

(Available to download at nickfox.co.uk)

I find the best way to document this information is on a spreadsheet (see the next document), as adding formulae makes it easy to keep up to date. However, it may be helpful to jot down initial calculations and thoughts here, together with any questions you may want to ask your financial advisor.

This snapshot is intended to show your monthly income, expenditure and positive (or negative) cash flow and allow you to calculate your personal net worth.

Income

Salary (weekly/monthly/annual):

Guaranteed bonus:

From stocks/shares/dividends:

Other income:

Expenditure

Credit/Store cards:

Loans:

Mortgage repayments:

Home expenses

Utilities:

Phone(s):

Broadband:

Insurance:

Personal expenses

Food/drink:

Car(s):

Clothing:

Entertainment:

Gym membership:

Other memberships:

Other monthly expenses/allowances:

Assets

Properties owned & value:

Investments:

Cars owned outright:

Savings:

Cash in bank:

Other assets:

Liabilities

Outstanding mortgages:

Credit card balances:

Personal loans:

Other loans (car, furniture, etc.):

Monthly cash flow = income less expenditure
£

Personal net worth = assets less liabilities
£

PERSONAL FINANCIAL SNAPSHOT

(Monthly figures)

INCOME		ASSETS	
Salary/wage		Value of properties owned	
Guaranteed bonus			
Stocks/shares			
Dividends			
Property		Investments	
Other...			
		Cars owned outright	
Total income	**£0**	Savings	
		Cash in bank	
EXPENDITURE		Other assets	
Credit cards			
		Total assets	**£0**
Store cards			
		LIABILITIES	
Loans		Outstanding mortgages	
Mortgage repayment			
Gas			
Electric		Credit card balances	
Water			
Council Tax			
Home insurance			
Phone line		Store card balances	
TV package			
Broadband			
Car insurance		Personal loans	
Car Tax		Other loans	
Car servicing			
Groceries			
Clothing		**Total liabilities**	**£0**
Entertainment			
Gym membership		**PERSONAL NET WORTH**	**£0**
Other			
Total expenditure	**£0**		
MONTHLY CASH FLOW	**£0**		

Notes for financial advisor…

PART TWO:

THE HMO MODEL

This second part gives an overview of the HMO market within the private rental sector, including letting to students, and looks at the specific characteristics of HMOs – what constitutes an HMO and what national and local authority legal requirements and standpoints may affect whether you can operate an HMO in a certain area. It highlights some of the things you will need to consider and investigate in your chosen location in order to establish whether you will be able to move forward with your plans there, or whether you will have to look at buying somewhere else.

Chapter 2 of 'HMO PROPERTY SUCCESS':

The HMO model (Part 1)

HMO (āch'ĕm-ō') *n.* Abbreviation for House in Multiple Occupation: a property shared by at least 3 tenants, forming more than 1 household*, where the tenants share toilet, bathroom or kitchen facilities.
(as defined by www.gov.uk)

(*A household consists of either a single person or members of the same family who live together. It includes people who are married or living together and people in same sex relationships.)

Investing in HMOs is by far the best way to maximise rental income and monthly profit from buy to let. There are some exceptions, such as luxury homes and corporate lets in capital cities, but, by and large, buying properties in areas where rental accommodation is in high demand (see Chapter 5) and letting the rooms to individual tenants will generate two to three times the amount of rental income that you could achieve by letting it as a single unit. Yes, the associated costs are higher and it takes more work to manage, but the rental income certainly makes the extra effort worthwhile.

To give you an example… By the start of 2007, I had a decent sized portfolio of properties, but all were let as single units and, while the portfolio as a whole was profitable, one four bedroom detached house was losing me money each month. It was a lovely property, so, rather than simply cutting my losses and selling, I decided to create two extra bedrooms and turn it into a six bedroom HMO. The rental income jumped from £1,200 to £2,500 a month and the liability in the portfolio suddenly become its most profitable asset. That was my 'light bulb' moment, when I realised how much more profitable my portfolio could be.

Just a little word of warning: if you're now thinking of doing the same to an existing portfolio, stagger the conversions. While it was, ultimately, undoubtedly the right move to turn 20 of my properties into HMOs, what I didn't quite think through was the practicality of doing all 20 at the same time I think I was so overcome with excitement that I had 'discovered' this brilliant new business model, that I didn't properly think through the logistical or financial implications. Having all those properties not generating any income for nearly two months, on top of the cost of the necessary refurbishment, meant things were very tight – not to mention hectic for quite a few months. I'd certainly take my time if I did it again.

A lot of people still think of HMOs as 'student housing', but the model has come a long way in the last ten years and the vast majority of both established and new investors I meet are letting rooms to young adults in full time employment. Some fall into the 'young career professionals' category; others are working in bars, restaurants and shops. Many are on short term contracts and find it much more convenient to rent a room than a flat for a few months, as landlords usually request a 12 month rental commitment; some tenants will rent a room in the same property for years.

As the landlord of an HMO, you are typically responsible for:

- Providing and maintaining all fixtures, fittings and white goods
- Fully furnishing the property – including kitchen/dining equipment, but not linen
- Paying council tax and utility bills (excluding telephone)
- Providing and paying for broadband
- Providing a regular cleaning service for the communal areas

…in other words, you're providing the kind of accommodation your tenants might expect if they were living at home with their parents – in some cases, better accommodation The tenants seem to like the ease of all inclusive rent and, because many of them are of a similar age, it's often a good social environment for them. (See Chapter 9 in PART SIX for more detailed information on refurbishment and getting a property 'ready to rent'.)

The cons

I'm going to start with the downsides, or the more challenging aspects of operating HMOs, because there's no getting away from them and if you're going to get into this business, you need to understand exactly what lies ahead.

Bad press. One of the things you will always come up against is the preconception that multi let houses mean cheap and nasty accommodation, run by landlords who care more about making money than the wellbeing of their tenants, packing as many people as they can into one house for the sake of profit. Like it or not, there's a popular feeling out there that 'decent' landlords let properties as one unit, rather than room by room, and choosing to go down the HMO route is rather un savoury.

Unfortunately, yes, there are some landlords who don't comply with either property regulations or their legal and moral obligations to their tenants. They don't look after their investments and, as the standard of accommodation goes down, so does the quality of tenants. Then, because of the media's love of a good horror story, it's these tales of 'slum landlords' and tenants treating properties like 'doss houses' and running cannabis factories that people hear about.

So, although the kind of HMOs I'm talking about running are nothing like that, nor the old stereotype of 'student accommodation' and, thankfully, the number of good, professional landlords is increasing, you need to be prepared for a less than enthusiastic reaction when you tell people what you're doing. My advice is to talk as little as possible about it until you're up and running, because it's very easy to be put off by 'advice' from people who have very little relevant understanding or experience.

Heavy management demands. Ask any investor not currently investing in HMOs why they're not, and the first thing out of their mouth will probably be, "It's far too much hassle dealing with all the tenant problems." A group of unrelated people living in a house together can sometimes result in more disagreements and more (often petty) complaints, and you'll undoubtedly get far more maintenance issues than you would renting an unfurnished property to a family. You need tact, diplomacy, strength of character, a good team of tradesmen and the willingness and ability to respond quickly to issues.

Admin. With multiple tenants come multiple sets of paperwork and an increased number of phone calls, viewings, move ins and move outs.

Tighter legal requirements. HMOs fall under very specific licensing, planning, health and safety, building and letting regulations and laws. There has been a lot of change in policy over recent years, so you need to make sure that you not only adhere to the policies and requirements in force at the time you acquire and let your HMO, but that you stay up to date and compliant. (See Chapter 3, PART THREE, for more details.)

Staff. If you want to build a significant portfolio of HMOs, there's no question you'll need to employ a team of people to help you run it. You could probably manage between two and five houses on your own, but after that it can quickly become a full time job. And going back to why you want to invest, I bet, 'because I want to be a property manager' wasn't anywhere on your list So you'll need to be prepared and able to hire and manage staff of your own.

The good news is that, while all this is time consuming and requires organisation and attention to detail, it can all be systemised and outsourced to a small team, under your control. I'll stress again that you must understand this is a property business and you'll need business skills to run it.

The pros

The upsides of investing via the HMO model echo the key reasons I gave in the last chapter for why I invest in property as an asset class. To reiterate, HMOs offer the most reliable, tangible and profitable form of investment I've been able to find.

CASH FLOW I haven't met a single investor who's operating HMOs for any reason other than cash flow and profit HMOs involve far more work and the running costs are higher than for single lets, but the rental income is up to three times as much as you would get from letting the property as a single unit. That means both your yield and profitability tend to be significantly higher than average buy to let figures. Two reasons why the cash flow is so good are:

a. Voids don't have the same impact as with single lets. As a general rule of thumb, in an average bedroom HMO, rooms 1 to 4 cover your costs and rooms 5 and 6 are your profit. The likelihood of having more than one room empty at a time is extremely low, so even if you lose a tenant, you're still profitable. Compare that to losing a tenant in a single let, where you have to cover all the property costs yourself until you find a new tenant.
b. Virtually recession proof rental income. When times are hard, people cut costs and an all inclusive room rental makes it easy for people to budget and much cheaper and less hassle than renting a whole flat. I haven't suffered any drop in tenant demand since the credit crunch hit and have consistently operated at 98% occupancy.

Flexibility of investment. Because HMOs tend to be larger properties, the building usually offers the potential to be reconfigured as/when the demand (for rental or sale) changes. Most of the HMOs I've bought have been family houses that I've then reconfigured, by way of stud walls and adding bathroom facilities, so they could easily be turned back into family homes if there was a high demand for those.

Similarly, there may be the option to separate the house into separate flats or adapt it to accommodate those with disabilities or the elderly. Buying things that offer a good degree of flexibility means you give yourself the best chance of maximising profitability into the future.

Helping with the housing shortage. Most investors I know have an element of philanthropy in their overall life plan and, while I'm not for a minute claiming to be investing purely for the good of others, the simple fact is that by providing good quality accommodation and maximising the occupancy potential of some of the existing housing stock, we're helping. The Government needs more good private sector landlords offering decent, affordable housing.

The market for HMOs

Landlords who have experience of letting HMOs might feel that they can skip this section, but for those entering the market for the first time, what follows will give an overview of the factors to weigh up before buying an HMO in a particular area.

Some new landlords purchase an HMO as a financial investment, others inherit a property and want to achieve a long term income, and some may become reluctant landlords as they cannot sell their home but must move on.

HMO landlords should consider several market factors to make the most of a rental property.

By thinking about the whole rental market before jumping on the ladder, landlords can ensure they have the best possible plan for long term returns that meet their business and financial expectations while satisfying tenant needs.

These take into account factors like location and type of property and who the tenants are likely to be before making any financial commitment.

The argument for letting HMOs

The business premise for an HMO is quite simple - an HMO maximises cash flow as landlords can let by the room rather than trying to find a single tenant to take on the entire house.
 These properties have massive appeal to students and young professionals.

For example, take the rent for a three bedroom house let on a standard tenancy agreement at £700 per month. The maximum rent in a year, assuming no rental voids, is £8,400 (£700 x 12 months).

Convert the same property into an HMO and then let each bedroom at £80 each for exclusive occupation of their room and shared facilities. The maximum rental in a year - again, assuming no voids - is £80 x 3 bedrooms x 52 weeks = £12,480.

The figures are simplistic but demonstrate how HMO lettings are more profitable than single tenancy lettings. In the above example, if a reception room could also be utilised as a bedroom, the annual rental income would increase to £16,640, bringing in twice as much as letting the property as a single unit.

HMO letting introduces economies of scale. The workload is about the same for the landlord, but return on investment increases.

Furthermore, young professionals renting at a high quality, well managed HMO are likely to stay and look after the property just as much as a couple or family rents a buy to let home.

HMOs can present a profitable investment for landlords and a welcoming, stable home for tenants.

Size and future of market

The HMO lettings market has seen an upward trend in recent years and is expected to continue to grow.

With large deposits and mortgages out of reach for many young professionals, the need for private rented accommodation remains strong. Singles who do not wish to live with a partner often look to a shared house to help them manage their finances and maintain an active social life.

Data from the Department for Communities & Local Government's English Housing Survey 2011/12 shows strong levels of demand in the private rented sector.

The most recent figures from DCLG reveal that 17.4% or 3.84 million households were private rental accommodation last year.

For landlords, the size and expected growth in demand in the private rental market can mean strong competition among tenants for their properties, giving them peace of mind that they will rarely struggle to let rooms. With the picture expected to remain the same in coming years, buy to let investments are a good choice for many.

The survey also shows that out of the 3.84 million private renters, 26.5% are single households, which gives a market size of 1,017,600 people.

Around 23,000 single private renters are over 65 years old, leaving just under 995,000 singles of working age.

Types of HMO market

If the property is already owned and the aim is to switch to an HMO, then type and location pre determine the market.

Not all properties make good HMOs. The most important factor for a letting property that is already owned is whether the location suits tenant demand. If not, the time and money spent on conversion is likely to go to waste.

Property investors buying for the first time or adding to a portfolio must take some time to consider the market in the area they are considering, looking at factors such as:

- Demand and supply. Inner city locations may have a surplus of rented accommodation and competition between landlords is higher. In the suburbs, the opposite may be true

- Market characteristics. Is the property suitable for an HMO and the market it intends to serve?

- Potential for growth. Is this an area where demand for rented properties is expected to rise? Will new housing developments take people away from the rental market and into home ownership?

These issues will shape the rental market and influence how attractive the property is as an HMO, the level of rent expected and the likely tenants.

Of course, the potential for rental income, the location and standard of accommodation will also affect the investment cost, which could be a deciding factor for landlords.

The other element to consider is the tenant demographic. Broadly, the market splits into five types:

- People on benefits
- Students
- Working tenants
- Professionals
- Luxury or corporate lets
-

Again, if the property is already owned, then the tenant market may be predetermined by the location, but for those looking to buy, the people targeted as tenants can help with decisions such as location, rents and standards of decor.

Each group of renters also brings their own characteristics. Students move house at the end of each academic year, which can lead to lengthy voids. Young professionals often move around for work, especially if they are contractors, and if several decide to move out at the same time, major cash flow problems can ensue.

These differences in rental groups also go right down to the level of wear and tear you can expect in your property. Shift workers may be in the property for long periods of the day and students may hold more parties than young professionals, however, they will all demand good quality accommodation that is well managed and safe to live in.

Factors influencing the HMO market

In some areas, the simple lack of high quality rental properties makes the market highly competitive. Urban locations can be lucrative for landlords with the right properties, but many city centres are flooded with newly built apartment blocks all vying for the same market and pushing down rents.

For landlords letting HMOs to students, most universities only have enough halls of residence to house first year students, and private halls provide even fewer beds.

In major university cities, thousands of students can be searching for a new home each year, making this a lucrative market.

However, some downsides affect the market as well.

HMOs are subject to planning and licensing by local authorities and some councils are cracking down on the number of shared houses.

Some factors beyond the control of a property investor affect the popularity and profitability of HMOs. Local planning strategies, rental markets and government policy can exert sudden changes on the market, for example, the legislation coming into force in late 2014 requiring all letting agents be members of an ombudsman.

Here are a couple of points to bear in mind when looking for a suitable HMO property:

- Planning permission. Many councils manage the number of HMOs in some neighbourhoods with Article 4 directions (see page 41) that limit the number of shared houses for rent, while larger homes require mandatory planning permission and licensing.

- Housing benefits. Universal credit caps the amount of housing benefit paid and the type of homes that many singles aged under 35 can rent.

Planning to open an HMO

Once you have decided on the target tenant market, the next step is to plan buying a property. Don't forget, rental properties are an investment, so need to turn a profit in order to be viable.

You can't afford to leave the investment to chance, so you must put together an accurate and realistic HMO viability business plan that includes:

- Property asset value and loan to value ratio of the mortgage
- The cost and repayment period of the mortgage
- Interest on the mortgage
- Investment required for refurbishment and to ensure the property meets HMO regulations
- The cost of any management or specialist services
- Financing for on going maintenance and repair costs
- Utility bills
- How much rent will be charged
- Allowances for void rental periods

You must be clear on the amount of initial capital required and be able to project ongoing income and expenditure as accurately as possible. Once you have those figures, you will be able to calculate the expected profit and return on your capital invested, which will allow you to compare properties with each other and also see how property stacks up against other investment options.

This information is best recorded on a spreadsheet – here is a suggested template, which can also be downloaded at nickfox.co.uk:

HMO VIABILITY ANALYSIS TEMPLATE

Asking Price	£244,500
Purchase Price	£230,000
Current market valuation	£248,000

Legal & Purchase costs

Legal Fees	£800
Mortgage Broker Fees	£400
Valuation Fees	£350
Searches & other admin costs	£550
Stamp duty	£2,300
Total Legal & Purchase	**£4,400**

Deposit	**£23,000**

Additional capital investment

Basic refurbishment costs	£10,000
Fire / Health & safety fixtures & fittings costs	£3,000
Gas & electrical certification costs	£500
Licensing costs	£500
Furnishing	£4,000
White & electric goods	£1,500
Total additional capital	**£19,500**

Mortgage payments until rented (c. 6 weeks)	**£1,173**

TOTAL INITIAL CAPITAL INVESTMENT	**£48,073**

KEY INVESTMENT PERFORMANCE INDICATORS

Gross Yield	13.42%
Net Yield	4.88%
Return on capital invested	23.36%

Mortgage (interest ony)

Product	
Loan to value	90%
Mortgage interest rate	4.84%
Amount borrowed (excl. fees)	£207,000
Total borrowing (incl. fees)	£210,000
Mortgage term (years)	20
Total interest over term	£203,280

Monthly Expenditure

Mortgage repayment	£847
Council tax	£145
Insurance	£29
Electric	£77
Water	£48
Gas	£88
TV licence	£11
Phone line rental	£13
Broadband	£100
5% void allowance	£139
Bookkeeping	£50
Gardener	£15
Cleaning	£125
Misc expenses allowance	£150
Total monthly expenditure	**£1,837**

Monthly pre-tax profit	**£936**

Annual pre-tax profit	**£11,231**

Key figures if employing mangement company

Management (12%)	£333	12%
Monthly expenditure	£2,170	
Monthly pre-tax profit	£603	
Annual pre-tax profit	£7,237	
Net Yield	2.92%	
Return on capital invested	15.06%	

Room income	Average: £106.67	
	No.	Weekly income
Double @ 140		£0.00
Double @ 120	2	£240.00
Double @ 115		£0.00
Double @ 110	2	£220.00
Double @ 105		£0.00
Double @ 100	1	£100.00
Double @ 95		£0.00
Single @ 90		£0.00
Single @ 85		£0.00
Single @ 80	1	£80.00
Single @ 75		£0.00
Single @ 65		£0.00
Total weekly income		**£640.00**
Total monthly income		**£2,773.33**

The key in all these areas is realism. Landlords should allow around a 5% void rate for vacant rooms and the turnaround time between tenancies.

Don't forget furniture will need replacing now and then, walls will need painting and soft furnishings updating because of general wear and tear.

Landlords must avoid the tendency to plan just for the first few months when the cash investment is high.

This is undoubtedly a tough period to get over, with bills to pay and no rent coming in, but other challenges will continue to crop up down the line, such as if a large repair is needed or a tenant falls into rent arrears, so it's important to maintain a 'sinking fund' to cover these periodical costs.

Commitments such as mortgages and utility rates do not stop if the rent is not coming in.

How many HMOs?

The short answer is: no one knows. One of the problems is many councils have failed to keep accurate licensing records and a report Evaluation of the Impact of HMO Licensing and Selective Licensing, published in January 2010 by the Department of Communities and Local Government, revealed a shambolic picture of HMO management by councils.

Some of the headline statistics included:

- England has about 56,000 HMOs needing a licence. Most are in London, Yorkshire and Humberside. About 93% of councils have received at least one HMO licence application, while 75% have had up to 100. Only 11 councils processed more than 500 HMO licences.

- In June 2008, a survey of councils reported 22,648 mandatory HMO applications received and 16,399 licences issued. The survey estimates that 23,000 HMO properties requiring a licence do not have one.

- A third of councils (32%) reported HMO licensing avoidance, including reducing occupancy levels to below the mandatory licensing threshold and converting HMO properties into self contained flats. How many landlords avoid licensing is hearsay, as councils do not keep the appropriate records to support the figures

- Most councils (83%) thought they had fewer than 100 HMOs where landlords had not applied for a licence. A fifth of councils thought they might have more than 100.

- Over 50% of councils reported a positive effect on the quality of accommodation from HMO licensing.

- Many HMOs needing licences are in areas with high student populations. All 11 councils receiving more than 500 applications for HMO licences have significant student populations.

- Councils consider the most likely HMO tenants as the unemployed (29%) followed by students (22%). Migrant workers were the next most likely tenants in 28 (13%) council areas.

Some tenants experienced significant improvements to their standard of housing from licensing, including better fire safety, kitchen and bathroom facilities. Others were unaware of any changes and had problems with damp and a lack of fire safety.

Student Letting Facts and Figures

Providing homes for students is a big market for HMO landlords – and following the lead of some of the corporates, providing student housing saves 'reinventing the wheel'.

Many companies, like Unite, the UK's largest corporate student housing provider with around 44,000 beds, build developments at transport hubs that service more than one university or college.

That removes their reliance on the continuing popularity and successful education policies of a single institution. Unite also maximises income by looking for other letting opportunities in the university summer holidays. During the London 2012 Olympics, the firm made a cool extra £1 million by letting rooms to games officials.

Students – the numbers

The worry for student landlords was the hike in tuition fees at English universities from £3,000 a year to £9,000 a year, at the start of 2012 /2013 academic year.

The fear was that soaring costs would deter students from signing up for degree courses, but the boom in further education seems to have carried on unabated.

Although applications from England were down around 27,000, the slack was taken up by more wealthy students from overseas snapping up the vacant places.

According to the Higher Education Statistics Agency (HESA), Britain had just fewer than 2.5 million students at 158 universities and colleges in the 2012/2013 academic year, with almost 500,000 came from overseas.

Adding up the capacity of all Britain's university halls of residence and corporate student housing providers, private landlords offer homes to around two thirds of the country's students.

London outstrips the rest of the country as the main destination for students with a fifth (20%) living in the capital. Manchester snatches second place with 4%.

The top 10 cities house almost half (47%) of all Britain's students and offer 76 of the nation's higher education institutions.

As a market indicator, Oxford, one of the oldest and most sizeable universities has 44,000 students at two universities – with the council reckoning the city has just over 5,000 HMOs.

Top 10 Cities By Student Numbers

City	Students from:			Total	% of total of all students
	UK	EU	Other		
UK total	1,815,250	128,525	299,670	2,243,445	100%
London	341,205	40,225	79,400	460,830	20.54%
Manchester	79,515	4,940	12,410	96,865	4.32%
Birmingham	58,625	3,295	10,655	72,575	3.23%
Leeds	56,465	2,140	6,385	64,990	2.90%
Glasgow	54,015	3,670	7,105	64,790	2.89%
Nottingham	51,905	2,510	9,145	63,560	2.83%
Sheffield	51,980	1,775	9,370	63,125	2.81%
Cardiff	49,165	2,245	10,535	61,945	2.76%
Edinburgh	41,005	6,410	10,435	57,850	2.58%
Liverpool	46,645	1,445	6,690	54,780	2.44%
Totals	830,525	68,655	162,130	1,061,310	
Totals as % of all students	45.71%	3.78%	8.93%	58.46%	

SOURCE: HESA

Exactly what is an HMO?

'House in Multiple Occupation' is a specific planning term that was introduced in the Housing Act 2004, which has seen some modification over the years. Many property investors are confused about HMOs, as the term is not defined in housing law, only under planning legislation.

The easy way of thinking of an HMO is as a property with a single front door where the tenants then have their own locked living space inside, but share facilities, such as kitchens and bathrooms. Blocks of flats are not HMOs because the living space is self-contained. HMOs come in two types, with different planning rules for large and small:

Large HMOs

A large HMO is a property lived in by six or more unrelated tenants who share facilities, or a property with fewer than six tenants but with three or more floors. Basements and attics count as storeys if they have living accommodation. Large HMOs will almost always require a licence. (See Part 4 of the course for more detailed information on licensing.)

Counting storeys to determine if a property is an HMO was considered in a case at the High Court, London. In *Islington Council v Unite Group [2013] EWHC 508 (Admin)*, the judges decided the HMO unit must comprise the three storeys, rather than the building the HMO happens to be in.

A two storey HMO with up to five sharers is not an HMO that requires mandatory licensing.

Property investors must apply for planning permission before renting out a large HMO.

Small HMOs

A small HMO is a home lived in by three to five unrelated tenants sharing facilities, in a property of two floors or fewer – basically, a 'standard family home'. Small HMOs do not always need planning permission – you only make an application if the council has an 'Article 4 direction' (see page 41)

Note: HMO laws are different in England, Scotland and Wales. This manual only deals with planning rules and legal issues in England.

Testing if a property is an HMO

Before looking at the planning rules that apply to different types of HMO, the first step is checking out if the property actually slots in to the new regulatory system. Three tests are applied to the building to confirm whether it is an HMO.

Test 1 – The Standard Test This looks at how many people live in a building, their relationships and basic living standards. This test defines an HMO as:

- A building or part of a building
- Comprising one or more rooms that are not self contained flats
- Where three people live as more than one household
- The living space is the main home of the people staying there
- The living space is not used for any other purpose
- Rents or are payable or other consideration is provided by at least one person living in the house

AND

- Two or more of the households share or lack some or all basic amenities

WHERE

 "Self contained" is if people living in the self contained accommodation do not share basic amenities with anyone else

"Basic amenities" are a toilet, a bath, shower, sink or a kitchen

"Household" are people of the same family living together, including:

- Couples who are married or living together
- Relatives living together including grandparents, parents, uncles, aunts, sisters, brothers, children (including stepchildren), grandchildren, nephews, nieces and cousins
- Foster children living with their foster family
- Domestic staff living rent free with the family they work for.

Test 2 – The Self Contained Test

This test looks at a flat within a block to determine if a specific flat meets the criteria for HMO regulation. A self contained flat is an HMO if:

- The living space is part of a building containing a toilet, personal washing facilities and cooking facilities for exclusive use of the occupants

AND

- Two or more households share the flat
- The flat is the main residence of everyone living there
- The flat is only used as living accommodation
- At least one person pays rent or some similar financial consideration for living there
- At least two of the households lack or share basic amenities

Don't forget, a self contained flat is not an HMO by definition, but can qualify as an HMO if the conditions of the standard test are met.

Test 3 - The Converted Building Test

This test is designed to ensure that people living in a converted building are not at risk from fire or other hazards as a result of the conversion.

A building or a part of a building meets the converted building test if:

- It is a converted building
- The building has living space other than a self contained flat or flats
- Two or more households share the building
- The building is the main residence of everyone living there
- The building is only used as living accommodation
- At least one person pays rent or some other consideration for living there

WHERE

"Converted building" means a building or part of a building that has had alterations to the interior to create living space

"Self contained flat" means living space that has basic amenities available for the exclusive use of the people living there.

Article 4 directions explained

Planning rules are complicated; article 4 directions do nothing to make them clearer for property owners.

An article 4 direction is made under The Town and Country Planning (Use Classes) (Amendment) (England) Order 2010.

The principle behind an article 4 direction is a 'permitted development order'. These orders let property owners carry out certain improvements without the need for planning permission, such as adding an extension or building a garage, providing the new work does not exceed certain specifications.

An article 4 direction takes away permitted development rights in a specific area, such as a conservation area.

Many councils take on these powers to limit the numbers of HMOs in certain neighbourhoods. England has around 190 councils, about a third of which limit the number of new small HMOs with an article 4 direction.

The direction can apply to a neighbourhood, postcode area, local government ward or the whole town or city.

To find out if any proposed new small HMO needs planning permission, ask the local planning authority or check their web site.

Small HMO change of use

When a planning authority takes on article 4 powers, any small HMO is deemed to have retrospective planning permission.

However, if the property owner switches from shared letting to a single let and then wants to switch back to a small HMO, planning permission is needed.

The rule of thumb is switching from a small HMO to another use does not need planning permission, but switching from any other use back to a small HMO does.

Taking in lodgers

Taking one or two lodgers into your home is not running an HMO. Planning permission is not needed.

Watch for the planning trap of moving in a third lodger. This could make the property an HMO and if the home is in a neighbourhood subject to an article 4 direction, planning permission may be needed.

Buildings that are not HMOs

Housing law exempts a number of buildings from the need for HMO licensing:

Persons not forming a single household A single household excludes members of the same family or the main owners employ others in specific jobs:

- Au Pair
- Career or nurse
- Chauffeur
- Nanny or governess
- Gardener
- Secretary or personal assistant
- Cook or maid
- Cleaner
- Butler

Only or main residence
A property is not an HMO if it:
- is a refuge
- is housing for a migrant or seasonal workers, where the accommodation forms part of the 'contract' of employment in the UK, and the building is provided by the employer or agent
- the property houses asylum seekers or their dependents.

Buildings regulated by other Acts
A number of laws regulate buildings, such as homes for children, hospitals and prisons, but they are never classed as HMOs that need a licence.

Buildings occupied by the owners

- Homes lived in by the owner and their household, and no more than two other people who are not part of the household, unless their job excludes them from the calculation. (This is the section that can catch homeowners with three or more lodgers.)
- Any building occupied only by two people sharing.

CHECKLIST

Understanding the HMO model

☐ Understood the characteristics that define a property as an HMO

☐ Understood the difference between student HMOs and renting rooms to working adults

☐ Appreciated the downsides as well as the benefits, and really considered whether you're able and prepared to deal with them

☐ Considered again whether the 'pros' will satisfy your goals and objectives

☐ Put together an initial financial template for costs involved - projected profit - ROI (go to nickfox.co.uk to download a spreadsheet template)

☐ Researched local council's attitude to HMOs and discovered whether Article 4 Direction applies

☐ Researched demand in your area:

   ☐ Spoken to local college/university accommodation office

   ☐ Searched for 'rooms wanted' v 'rooms to let' on spareroom.co.uk and uk.easyroommate.com

   ☐ Spoken to local letting agents

PART THREE:

HMO INVESTMENT FINANCIALS

Here, we look at financing your HMO investment, from the deposit, purchase costs and securing a mortgage, to the costs you will incur refurbishing, getting the property ready to rent and maintaining it on an on going basis. We also look at how to assess the amount of rent you should be charging. This part begins with one of the most important elements of investing in HMOs: how to work out whether a property will make a good investment. Also covered are property surveys and reports, which represent not only a cost to you, but also form part of your investment viability due diligence.

Chapter 3 of 'HMO PROPERTY SUCCESS': The financials

Choosing how to finance your HMO investments is a major decision. There are various different options that you'll hear people talking about – great mortgage deals, joint ventures, lease options, etc. – but, fundamentally, which route you take will depend on four key factors:

1. How much capital you have
2. The bank's willingness to lend to you
3. Your attitude to risk
4. Your ability to find the right people and build good relationships with them

Before I go any further, I need to make one thing very clear: 'No money down' (NMD) deals do not exist. They used to, but regulations have tightened since the credit crunch hit and I haven't found a single NMD scheme since that is considered legal.

You cannot buy a property solely in your name without putting some of your own capital in and, if you do not fully disclose to a lender where the deposit funds are coming from you are committing mortgage fraud.

It's also mortgage fraud to not advise the lender of the actual price you're paying for the property (which is what some NMD schemes rely on), so if anyone suggests that to you, walk away from them. I'm amazed at how many people I meet who still think they can invest in property without any personal investment of money or time. Thankfully, the number of companies and self proclaimed 'gurus' out there suggesting it's possible seems to have fallen over recent years, but there are still quite a few rogues looking to take what little money people do have and give them little or nothing in return.

You need money behind you to invest in buy to let. As a rule of thumb, for every HMO you buy, you should budget for:

- a 25% deposit
- purchase costs of around £2,500 (solicitor's fees, disbursements, surveyor, etc.)
- Stamp duty of 1% of the purchase price (if purchase price is £250,000 or less; it's 3% if over £250,000 and 4% if over £500,000)
- somewhere between £5,000 and £30,000 for refurbishment (if required) and getting it ready to rent
- A 'contingency fund' to cover up to 2 months' initial mortgage payments and any other unexpected costs

So, if you're buying at £200,000 (a pretty average purchase price), you're going to need somewhere between £50k and £70k.

This is not a business for the under funded; it is a major investment and carries risk. The rewards are potentially very good, but it's certainly not something you should enter into lightly and that's why you need to work with a great team of professional advisors. Whoever you choose to help and advise you with financing (broker or IFA), should work together with your legal representative and wealth manager to make sure that what you buy and how you buy it is appropriate for your circumstances and in line with your objectives.

Risk

Property is considered a medium risk investment with the risk reducing the longer you plan to hold the investment for. HMO investing in particular offers the potential for great rewards, but with that comes greater risk.

"Progress always involves risks. You cant' steal second base
and keep your foot on first."
Frederick B. Wilcox

Getting a good ROI means taking on a lot of mortgage debt; having the right business structure in place to run your HMO portfolio involves employing and being responsible for other people; you stake your reputation on every deal you make and, if you choose to partner with another investor on joint ventures, you're not only risking your own money, but theirs as well. It all amounts to a lot of financial and emotional pressure and you need to seriously think about whether you're happy to accept that level of risk and responsibility.

The ultimate level of risk is massively reduced if you approach everything in a professional way, research and execute all your choices properly and become an excellent business manager. In short, it's up to you and dependent on the kind of person you are. If you're confident in your own abilities and are prepared to work hard at this business, you shouldn't need to worry unduly about the risks you're taking, because you'll know that you're doing everything possible to mitigate those risks.

"Risk comes from not knowing what you're doing."
Warren Buffett

Key financial risk factors and how you can insulate yourself against them:

Risk: capital values (house prices) going down.
Mitigate by: buying property at 10%+ below its 'true market'/surveyed value and considering it a long term investment.

Risk: rents falling.
Mitigate by: buying in areas where demand is currently high and likely to be high into the future.

Risk: void periods.
Mitigate by: providing good quality, well maintained accommodation at a fair market rent.

Risk: tenants causing damage to property.
Mitigate by: referencing tenants properly and insuring against malicious damage.

Risk: costs rising.
Mitigate by: testing your initial figures against a number of different cost base scenarios to make sure your investment still stacks up BEFORE you buy.

All of these factors can be tackled once you start researching your local property market, but the first risk you'll need to address is the risk that a lender takes in lending you mortgage finance.

Buy to let mortgages

Buy to let mortgages are different to residential mortgages in two main ways: the loan to value ratio is lower and is based primarily on the rental income potential of the property. I say 'primarily' because most (if not all) lenders will require you to have a personal income of at least £25,000 p/a before they'll consider you for a buy to let mortgage.

There are two steps you should take before approaching your financial advisor or mortgage broker:

1. Put together a personal financial statement: a document that lists all your assets, liabilities, income and expenditure, and that calculates your monthly cash flow and personal net worth. You can find templates if you do an online search.
2. Check your own credit score, via Experian or Equifax. As with any mortgage application, the lender will carry out a credit check on you, so make sure you're in

the best possible position and if there is anything adversely affecting your score, contact the companies directly and see what you can do to sort the problem out – something like a missed payment is sometimes simply a misunderstanding that can be rectified. It also helps your score if you've lived at the same address for more than three years, have been employed for a number of years and are on the electoral roll.

Once a lender has established you're credit worthy, how much they'll lend is usually calculated on the basis of the rental income (as verified by a surveyor) being at least 120% - 130% of the monthly repayment amount. And, as things currently stand, you will probably be looking at a 75% LTV ratio.

Example, assuming a requirement of 125% x monthly repayment:

Property value	£200,000
Borrowing required at 75%	£150,000
Monthly mortgage repayment	£625 (£150,000 x 5% ÷ 12)
(at 5% mortgage interest rate, interest only)	
Required rental valuation	£781 pcm (£625 x 125%)

Although the monthly rental income for an HMO is usually around £2,500+ pcm, most lenders won't accept a 'room rental' valuation, as they're always considering a worst case scenario and will err on the side of safety, i.e. you only being able to rent the property as a single unit.

So you need to look for the kind of property that would not only make a good HMO but also rent well as a single unit let, otherwise you may have to be prepared to accept a lower LTV and put in more of your own capital, and that's not going to give you as good a return as if you gear highly.

A caveat to the above is that you might need a specialist HMO mortgage – which you almost certainly will with a licensable HMO – so you'll need to discuss it thoroughly with your broker or IFA. Lenders will look at whether you're buying something that's already classed as an HMO and will also need full disclosure on how you intend to rent the property, so you must make sure that both you and your financial representative are declaring what's legally required.

One final thing you need to bear in mind is that lenders limit the number of buy to let mortgages an individual can have, so make sure that you thoroughly plan with your wealth manager, IFA and legal representative how to grow your portfolio legally and efficiently.

More creative ways of funding your investment…

I said at the start of the chapter that how you're able to finance your investments is dependent partly on finding the right people to work with and on your ability to build good relationships with those people. You'll only be able to embark on the more creative options if people trust you and you can prove to them that you know what you're doing, so there's no point in trying to approach investors for joint ventures (JVs) or put together a lease option or other 'creative purchase' proposition until you've got at least a couple of successful HMOs under your belt. In other words, there's no getting away from needing capital when you start out

I've done many JVs and partnering with other people has allowed me to grow my portfolio far more quickly and easily than I would otherwise have been able to. And every one of those JVs is a true partnership – we share the risk and the reward equally – which is how you need to approach these deals. Finding the right people to partner with, whose investment goals you can satisfy and vice versa, isn't a quick process and it's not something you can really put a timescale on. People buy into people, so make sure the buzz surrounding you is that you're a) good at what you do and, b) ethical and decent in all your business dealings.

Always do what you've said you'll do,
When you've said you'll do it.

Tax & wealth planning

This is an incredibly important area of investment in general, and property tax is its own world. You may already have a tax advisor, but do they have experience of working specifically with buy to let investors? How you're taxed on your property investments will depend on a number of factors, such as how they are legally owned, how you take income from them and what other businesses and income you have, and everyone's situation is different.

As I've already said, you need to make sure that your HMO portfolio sits properly within the context of your existing financial/tax affairs and that property is, in fact, the right investment vehicle for you. So, if you haven't already, start looking into getting specialist, tailored advice now.

'Stacking up' an HMO investment

No matter what type of property you opt for, the location and the letting market you aim to target, the figures must add up. The calculations you should make before putting in an offer will give you a very good indication of the likely returns and viability of your investment, so you can buy with confidence.

This first section takes you step by step through these formulas and calculations and shows how to apply them to your own property purchase, so you can see whether the deal 'stacks up'.

Calculating loan to value ratios and deposits

Loan to value (LTV) is the amount of mortgage borrowing a lender will advance against a property.

The amount is expressed as a percentage, such as 75% LTV. That means a bank or building society will consider a mortgage of up to 75% of the purchase price you agree with the owner, or the surveyor's valuation of the property, whichever is the lowest.

This is a key point to remember. You may think you have a bargain by agreeing a £100,000 purchase price against a property you think is worth £150,000, but the LTV rule means you can only borrow a maximum of 75% of what you pay, even if the property is worth more. So forget the idea that you could get a mortgage of £112,500 (75% of £150,000) and put the extra cash into your pocket. (That way of structuring a 'cash back' purchase was possible pre credit crunch, but has not been allowed since.)

The reverse also applies. A mortgage lender will only let you borrow a maximum of 75% of the surveyor's valuation even if you agree a higher buying price with the seller. Remember, the surveyor acts for the lender, to protect their loan against the property. Therefore, if you agree to buy for £100,000 but the valuation only comes back at £90,000, then the mortgage is 75% of £90,000 ((£67,500) and the difference comes as an extra deposit – although you should be able to agree a reduction in purchase price with the vendor, given that the property has been 'down valued' by a professional surveyor.

The average LTV is 75%, according to the Council of Mortgage Lenders, the bank and building society trade body, but some lenders offer higher and lower LTVs. You can either take the cash you have and work out the price you can afford to pay or you can take the buying price of a home and see how much capital you need to put into the deal.

Figuring out what you can afford

Working out the maximum purchase price, given your available capital

Let's assume you have £200,000 in the bank and want to buy an HMO. That capital will need to cover both the deposit and your costs, which include:

- Buying costs, such as stamp duty, survey and legal fees

- Lender's mortgage fees – although these can often be added to the loan without affecting the LTV

- Property refurbishment costs

- Furnishing costs

- Running costs until the property is let

- HMO licensing fees (as applicable)

- Cash reserve

Each of these costs will vary from property to property, but setting aside a third of your cash for these costs is not an unreasonable estimate. Say they come to around £66,000, that leaves £134,000 in your kitty for the deposit.

If the lender is offering 75% LTV, that £134,000 represents 25% of your budget. So, multiply £134,000 x 3 to find the mortgage at 75% LTV: £402,000. Add that amount to your £134,000 deposit and that gives you a maximum purchase price of £536,000.

The formula for calculating the price of a property you can afford from the amount of cash you have in the bank is:

((Total investment cash less costs) divided by (100 – LTV)) x 100

Taking our example above: ((£200,000 - £66,000) / (100-75)) x 100

that's: £134,000 / 25 = £5,360
£5,360 x 100 = £536,000

Working out the deposit from a property price

This is the reverse calculation. Following the example above, if you want to buy a property valued at

£528,000 and the maximum mortgage LTV is 25%, your deposit will be:

Purchase price x LTV%

In this case: £536,000 x 25% = £134,000

Rent cover explained

Rent cover is a nominal formula that banks and buildings societies use to calculate affordability for property investment loans. Although they might offer up to a maximum LTV, this is subject to rent cover supporting the loan.

If you see 'Rent cover 125%' on a mortgage deal, this means that the gross monthly rent should exceed the monthly mortgage repayment by 25%. Typically, lenders will work the figures on a 5% interest only mortgage rate, regardless of the actual rate of the loan.

So, rent cover at 125% for £402,000 of mortgage borrowing, as in our example, is worked out like this:

£402,000 x 5% annual mortgage interest = £20,100 per annum interest only repayment
£20,100 divided by 12 = £1,675 per month
£1,675 x 125% = £2093.75 minimum monthly rent

The formula for monthly rent cover is:

((Mortgage borrowing amount x interest rate %) divided by 12) x 125%

So, for a maximum 75% LTV mortgage, the property needs to generate a monthly rent of no less than £2093.75 a month. If the amount is lower, the maximum borrowing will adjust downwards. If the rent is higher, the maximum LTV remains the same.

Calculating mortgage borrowing from the rent

The reverse calculation of the above is the formula used to establish the maximum borrowing a lender is likely to offer:

((Total annual rent divided by rent cover rate) divided by mortgage interest rate) x 100

So, if the rent on the £536,000 property you are looking to buy is currently £1,450 a month, that's:

((17,400 / 125%) / 5%) x 100

i.e.: £1,450 x 12 = £17,400 annual rent
£17,400 / 125% = £13,920 maximum annual 5% mortgage interest payment
(£13,920 / 5) x 100 = £278,400 maximum mortgage borrowing

That would mean you would need to put in £249,600 capital in order to be able to buy the property. It simply doesn't stack up at that rent rate.

Chapter 2 of 'HMO PROPERTY SUCCESS' (Part 2): KPIs for HMOs

(Covered in more detail in Chapter 12 of the book; see PART EIGHT)

Whether you're running a portfolio of HMOs or single let properties, you have to be able to monitor and measure your investment against itself, other similar properties in the market and other investment options. You need to set up a system (I do it on Excel spreadsheets) to track income and expenditure, rental and capital values and occupancy figures. Those will allow you to assess your returns and see whether you're maximising those returns.

You need to be absolutely precise about the costs and rental income for each property. While that's something your bookkeeper should take care of for you on an on going basis, you must be able to calculate for yourself with a high degree of accuracy how profitable a property is likely to be, BEFORE you buy it. There are a lot of costs associated with buying and operating an HMO and you need a spreadsheet that breaks those down in detail so you can quickly calculate whether the monthly cash flow stacks up and how good a return you'll be getting on the capital you'll need to invest.

Returns can be measured in a number of ways, but I focus on three in my business: profit, return on investment (ROI) and yield.

Profit

Fundamentally, this is what keeps me, my lifestyle and my portfolio going – and I presume it's your main reason for going down the HMO route. In addition to monthly bills, you'll need to plough some of the rental income back into your investment, in the shape of maintenance and updates to fixtures, furnishings and the fabric of the property itself, but you should be building those costs into your budget, so that your 'profit' figure is, or could be, personal income.

Remember to include tax in your costings and revisit all the items on your income and expenditure spreadsheet on at least a monthly basis. Even small reductions in utility bills, a quarter of a percent reduction in mortgage interest and minor increases in rent can add up to a significant increase in profit across a portfolio of properties.

ROI

Annual Profit ÷ Total Capital Invested
= Annual Return On Investment

As a professional investor, ROI should be right up there with profit as a key measure. If your main investment goal is monthly income, you may be tempted to put more capital into your HMO in order to reduce your mortgage payments, but I don't think that's a smart move. I've already said that one of the main benefits of investing in property (versus other assets) is that you can leverage the bank's money and benefit from capital growth on not just your own money, but theirs as well. Investing as little of your own money as possible means that you'll be maximising the return on your own capital, essentially making your money work harder for you.

One of the main benefits of renting out rooms is that the rental income (and therefore profit) is maximised, so you can afford to gear highly. In time, you may be able to refinance so that there is less of your own capital left tied up in the property. If you're able to take all off the original capital out, you'll have an 'infinite' ROI: all the profit for no financial investment.

Example:

Annual rental income	£30,000
Annual costs	£18,000
Annual profit	£12,000
Total capital invested	£75,000
	(deposit, buying costs, refurbishment, furnishing, etc.)
Annual ROI	16% (£12k ÷ £75k)

Refinance after 5 years, withdrawing £50,000, to leave only £25,000 capital invested:
Annual ROI   48% (£12k ÷ £25k)

You can also add capital growth figures to rental income to gain an ROI figure for a period of time, e.g.

Original purchase price	£200,000
Capital invested	£75,000
Value after 5 years	£250,000
Capital growth	£50,000
Rental profit	£60,000 (£12k x 5 years)
Total profit over 5 years	£110,000
Annual ROI over life of investment	29.3% ((£110k ÷ 5) ÷ £75k)

Once you have your ROI figure/s, you can compare it/them to other investment returns and see how your HMOs are performing for you.

Yield

This is talked about as a headline figure by the media and many investors but, for me, it comes behind profit and ROI, and is simply an indication of how 'good' my investment choice is for the area. There are two key reasons why I don't rate it as highly as the other two as a measure of success:

a. National yield figures are usually either gross or don't even state whether they're gross or net – i.e. costs are often not factored in. And sometimes a figure stated as 'net' actually only takes into account the mortgage repayment, none of the other associated costs.
b. Yield doesn't take into account how much of your own capital has been invested, i.e. whether you're highly geared or own the property outright, your yield figure could be the same.

People calculate yield in slightly different ways, but the most common calculations are: rental income divided by the property's value (gross yield), and profit divided by the property's value (net yield).

To use the figures from the last example:

Purchase price	£200,000
Rental income	£30,000
Profit (income – costs)	£12,000 (£30k - £18k)
Gross yield	15% (£30k ÷ £200k)
Net yield	6% (£12k ÷ £200k)

The national average yield figure quoted tends to fluctuate between 4% and 5%. This is mainly based on single lets and is usually a gross figure. As a general rule, HMOs gross between two and three times the national average yield, and your net yield percentage should still outstrip the national gross.

Although a lot of the KPI data can be compiled by your property manager and bookkeeper as your business grows, you will have to be able to do it all yourself in the early days. I'd suggest that if you're not already familiar with this kind of data compiling and tracking, that you read some basic business administration books and make sure you understand how spreadsheet programs such as Excel can help you.

The most important thing with analysis and tracking tools is that you understand them and they're user friendly for you; what's perfect for one investor isn't necessarily the right format for another. Work out a system that suits you, so you can keep it up to date and won't waste time completing information that's not useful to you.

Make it personal

Remember that this is YOUR business. The key KPIs listed above are, in my opinion, the most important ones that will enable you to monitor and compare your investment, but there may be others that you'd like to add, according to your fundamental goals and objectives. KPIs don't have to simply be financial, so if spending more time with your children is something you'd like property investment to facilitate, then make that measurable and put it on your spreadsheet. Because if you're succeeding financially, but not in terms of lifestyle goals, it needs to be flagged up and put right as soon as possible. Regular KPI analysis will keep not only your business, but also YOU on track.

Setting the rent

Deciding how much to charge per room is relatively straightforward, but many landlords do struggle to make an objective calculation. You need to determine a fair and reasonable rent and make sure that it covers costs and generates the profit you want and expect, without pricing the property out of the market.

Set rents too high and you will put prospective tenants off, unless you have a special unique selling point, resulting in high voids; too low and you may attract the 'wrong' type of tenants and find yourself unable to cover your running costs.

It should be emphasized that, as long as your initial research has been thorough enough, you shouldn't ever find yourself in the position of having bought a property for which you cannot charge sufficient rent to turn a decent profit.

On purchase, you should be confident of the rental bracket and have worked your budget on the worst and best case scenarios. Once you are ready to market your property, it should then simply be a case of fine tuning the rent, according to current market conditions.

To find your 'break even' point, you need to know your costs, from mortgage payments and council tax to utility rates and extras, such as broadband. You may have to estimate some of these costs so, if you're unsure, err on the side of caution and use the highest potential figures.

Look at comparable HMOs within half a mile or so and assess how your property compares. And always ensure you are comparing like for like, so if you are offering a property furnished, do not look at prices for unfurnished properties, and if you plan to let to working adults, don't look at prices for student accommodation.

Mystery shopping rival HMOs

A good way of checking out if the rent you want to charge is at a competitive commercial rate is to speak to letting agents and to 'mystery shop' a couple of similar, local HMOs. This will enable you to properly see what other landlords are offering, the finish of the rooms and the rents they command.

When mystery shopping, have a checklist to make notes about:

- Size of the communal areas and rooms
- Whether the rooms are en suite
- Are utility bills, council tax, satellite TV and broadband included?
- Is there parking, a garden and storage space?
- Is the property close to campus/amenities/the city centre?
- The quality of the finish and furnishings
- Is gardening and cleaning included?

All these factors affect the rent as a positive or negative factor.

Budgeting for ongoing costs

Before setting the rent, you need to have some figures that show you how much an HMO is going to cost each year.

The way to look at this is by making assumptions. If you already let property, this is easier because you have some evidence to base your figures on.

If not, you need to make enquiries for some quotes – the checklist already mentions some of the key expenses, but you also have to look deeper in to the on going and recurring running costs, such as:

- Landlord insurance
- Mortgage interest

- Gas boiler and appliance servicing and safety certificates
- Electrical appliance testing
- Council Tax during voids
- Letting agent costs
- A contingency fund for repairs and rental voids
- Professional costs – if you are hiring a bookkeeper or accountant
- Service costs – TV, broadband, cleaning, gardening and the like
- Ground rent / service charges (if leasehold).

Working out a projected cash flow

Most businesses prepare a monthly cash flow forecast with two columns for each month – one for the estimated budget amounts and the other for actual cash spent on each expense.

Tracking spending on a monthly basis ensures the right amount of money is kept aside for running the business to avoid cash flow problems.

Here's a sample cash flow forecast:

	April 2013		May 2013		June 2013	
	Forecast	Actual	Forecast	Actual	Forecast	Actual
Income	£1,200	£1200	£1,200	£1,040	£1200	£1,120
Mortgage	-£350	-£350	-£350	-£350	-£350	-£350
Insurance	-£105	-£105	-£105	-£105	-£105	-£105
Boiler		-£250				
HMO licence			-£585			
Cash BF	£0	£0	£745	£495	£1,490	£1,080
Profit/Loss for month	£745	£495	£745	£585	£745	£665
Cash CF	£745	£495	£1,490	£1,080	£2,235	£1,745

Key:

Cash BF – Cash brought forward from the previous month

Profit/loss for month – Income less expenses

Cash CF – Cash carried forward to next month

The forecast figure is the how much the landlord estimated for income and expenditure each month, while the actual figures show what was really taken as rent, and spent.

For instance, in April the boiler needed a repair and replacement parts. In May, a couple of tenants left and the HMO licence needed paying.

Over three months, the landlord's cash flow was 20% less than expected.

This is a simplified cash flow for a property business, but shows that just estimating expenses is not enough landlords need to measure performance as well. Most portfolio landlords will have a cash flow for each property and a consolidated cash flow forecast for the portfolio that aggregates the figures.

Once you have a cash flow worked out for the year, you can calculate your break even point – the money you need to pay all the bills.

Compare that with the commercial rate for each room and multiply by the number of letting rooms and the difference should be your profit.

Utility bills & extra services

The tenancy agreement should specify who is responsible for paying the utility bills.

Sometimes one tenant is responsible for bills, and this means other sharers must arrange between them to split the costs and pay on time.

In HMOs, to make life easier, the landlord often pays the bills and includes the cost in the rent. The rent agreement can include a clause that gas and electricity costs that exceed a certain amount each month, or else must be paid on top of the agreed rent.

Also allow for automatic cost of living reviews if energy prices go up. Landlords or their agents should keep a copy of all bills.

The aim is to make sure tenants do not take advantage of fixed price utilities by consuming more energy than expected or benefitting by paying a lower price when costs go up.

Any other services provided – such as a cleaner or gardener, broadband, satellite or cable TV can also be bundled into the rent. This makes budgeting easier for tenants and your property more attractive.

HMO mortgages

Financing HMO property comes with different issues and restrictions to 'standard' buy to let mortgages.

On top of a deposit and a rent cover 'stress test' to ensure you can get a mortgage at the necessary level of borrowing, you must also consider the availability of funds for things such as refurbishments and furnishings, licensing fees and rental voids.

Landlords can apply for a mortgage and any additional funding either directly to lenders or through a broker. A broker is likely to charge a fee. Lenders will need to know personal, business and financial information, such as credit history, how much deposit is available, other income and the business plan for the rental property.

Mortgage terms: These vary between lenders. Terms of 15 to 25 years are not uncommon, but some offer up to 30 years. Often lenders cap mortgage terms according to the age of the borrower, so many will set the term to end when a borrower is no more than 65 or 70 years old.

How much to borrow: HMO investors need a realistic view of the income and expenses involved in running a property. The deal should be 'stand alone', i.e. able to fund and support itself. Diverting rents or income from elsewhere to make up shortfalls is not a good business strategy. While lenders must adhere to 'responsible lending' guidelines, so you should borrow responsibly.

Business plans: Lenders will look favourably on investors who have a well thought through business plan that demonstrate how they intend to professionally manage their HMO.

By showing that you appreciate the risks and opportunities, have looked into the marketability and rental demand for the property and know the potential for capital value increases and the future of your investment, you should find that lenders will be more amenable to offering a loan.

Banks and building societies are generally happy to lend money for buying leasehold flats and houses, but it is usually more complicated for landlords to borrow in order to buy former commercial properties to refurbish as HMOs.

In the case of leasehold properties, most lenders will want no less than 35 years left on the lease at any point, so anything less than an 85 year lease does not give a lot of room for selling on once two 25 year mortgage terms are added to the minimum 35 years.

There are several banks that will lend money specifically for HMO purchases. Some have quirky conditions and will not lend if the HMO has more than five or six bedrooms, the tenants are on benefits or the local authority has imposed selective or additional licensing.

Although HMO mortgages will come with permission to let, other mortgages may prohibit house sharing without permission from the lender. (See 'Permission to let' in PART 6)

Interest rates

Interest rates for buy to let mortgages are usually 0.5% to 1% above the Standard Variable Rate (SVR), which itself is usually 1% above the Bank of England base rate. This is because of the perceived additional risk of lending.

Fixed or variable rates?

A fixed rate mortgage has a set interest rate for a pre determined period. This gives landlords the advantage of knowing exactly how much their mortgage repayments will be month in, month out.

The fixed term can be anything from 12 months to 10 years. At the end of the fixed term, the mortgage reverts to the lender's standard mortgage rate for HMOs.

If the mortgage is cleared during the fixed term, a penalty is generally applied by the lender.

A variable rate mortgage has an interest rate that varies in line with the lender's mortgage rate. If this goes down, so do mortgage payments, but the opposite is also true, so landlords must be confident that they can cope with fluctuations.

Budgeting to buy an HMO

With all these figures in mind, you can set your budget. This will help determine the size and location of the property you can afford, so you can then tailor your searches accordingly.

Generally speaking, a deposit of 30% to 40% will be required in order to take advantage of the most competitive mortgage deals. Survey, legal costs and arrangement fees should be added onto this initial cash requirement.

Good business practice also dictates that pre letting costs should be worked into your budget. The mortgage and bills will have to be paid from the very first month, regardless of whether you get tenants in straight away. Then there are the costs of refurbishment, fixtures, fittings and furniture.

Keep your head when considering your options and ensure that your investment is viable and will work for you in the long term. This also means considering the 'what ifs', such as what if you had to sell for unforeseen reasons or what if all your tenants moved out in quick succession and it took weeks to find new ones.

Never go for the cheap property just because it is cheap. Go for the one that makes the most financial sense.

Tax-effective property ownership

Tax planning should always be addressed before buying a property. It can seem complicated but taking time at the start to assess the options and put a strategy in place will make things easier further down the line.

There are three options for how to purchase a property:

- Sole purchaser
- Buying as joint tenants
- Buying as tenants in common

Properties can have up to four joint owners under English law and specialist advice should be taken from accountants and solicitors before signing a contract.

Sole ownership: If buying on your own, you are the sole owner and any rental profits and capital gains belong solely to you for tax purposes.

Joint tenants: Each owner has an equal share and the percentages cannot be changed. Two owners have 50% each, three have 33.3% each and four have 25% each.

Tenants in common: Owners can choose to split the shares however they like, however unequal. This could be 1%:1%:1%:97% for four owners if they wish. If no specific share is allocated then ownership defaults to equal shares.

Tenants in common ownership allows owners to shift the income in order to save tax.

For unmarried partners, this fixing of shares beats capital gains tax, as switching later could result in HMRC making demands. For married partners, transfers of all or part of a property are exempt from capital gains tax, so shares can be set when necessary to cut tax bills.

Changing the ownership of a property will have tax implications, and they may not be immediately obvious. Stamp duty might also be due if a property is mortgaged and the value of shares being shifted is over the threshold.

Income tax

Each taxpayer splits the rental profits or losses pro rata, based on their ownership share. So if a property makes £5,000 rental profit and is owned 50:50, each pays income tax at their highest rate on £2,500 – their half of the profits. Those in the 40% tax band would pay £1,000 and those in the 20% band would pay £500.

A more effective system would be to alter the ownership to 80:20 in favour of the person who pays the lowest tax rate. This would make the profit shares £1,000 and £4,000, with 40% tax of £400 on the smaller share and 20% tax of £800 paid on the larger share.

Capital gains tax

If the couple from the above example sold their rental property for a £60,000 gain (after reliefs and allowances), the tax as 50:50 partners would be:

    £30,000 x 28% for the higher rate taxpayer = £8,400
    £30,000 x 18% for the lower rate taxpayer = £5,400
    Total capital gains tax bill = £13,800.

If the 80:20 split was in place, the adjusted payments are:

    £12,000 x 28% for the higher rate taxpayer = £3,360
    £48,000 x 18% for the lower rate taxpayer = £8,640
    Total capital gains tax bill = £12,000

(Tax is covered in more detail in PART NINE.)

Property surveys, reports valuations

Surveys give both buyer and lender information on whether the property is worth what's being paid for it. All lenders require a basic valuation but it is advisable to have a more detailed survey carried out to protect your own investment. This closer examination can highlight problems that the basic survey does not cover and gives landlords an accurate picture of the state and condition of the property.

If a survey finds any major problems then price renegotiations should take place.

The standard strategy is to give the owner a chance to put the problem right at their expense or to agree a cost and deduct that from the purchase price. Be aware that a lender may withdraw their mortgage offer if the survey shows serious issues.

Basic surveys cost around £600 and this can usually be added on to the loan amount. The fuller homebuyer's report will be around £500, and any specialist surveys to assess specific issues will be more still. But paying this out ahead of the purchase is a worthwhile investment if there are any doubts about the integrity of the building.

Building surveys

The building survey is the most comprehensive and costly survey. The surveyor will thoroughly check the property to examine the structure, condition and any faults.

Specialist surveys can also be carried out on issues such as damp or subsidence. The report is thorough, as the surveyor is legally obliged to disclose all their findings. The detail can seem off putting, particularly with the estimated cost of repair and maintenance work, but a worst case scenario is usually given and the information can help investors make an informed decision about the property.

A full structural survey can take some time to carry out and you may have to wait around two weeks for the findings. The cost is usually up to £1,000, but will depend on the price and age of the house.

Homebuyer reports

The homebuyer report was introduced by the Royal Institution of Chartered Surveyors (RICS) in 2009, following market research, and was designed to be user friendly with little technical jargon.

The results are colour coded for easy understanding:

- Condition Rating 1 (green) - No repair needed

- Condition Rating 2 (amber) - Defects that need repair or replacing, but are not considered serious or urgent.

- Condition Rating 3 (red) - Defects that are serious and need urgent repair

Basic valuation

All lenders will require a basic property valuation to ensure they do not lend more than the property is worth and that if it needs to be repossessed and sold, they will get their money back.

The mortgage lender commissions the valuation, as it is for their interest, but the buyer has to pay for it.

The value of the property is calculated by comparing it with similar properties nearby and taking into account factors such as age, condition and location.

The valuation rules are set out by the RICS and followed by all valuers, so, although the price put on a property may vary a little between different valuers, their figures should certainly be in the same ballpark.

If the property is valued at less than the purchase price, the mortgage offer may be withdrawn or the amount of borrowing reduced. If work needs doing, the lender may keep some of the money as a 'retention', with that money being released on completion of the specified repairs.

This valuation takes around half an hour to carry out and costs between £100 and £300, depending on the price of the house.

CHECKLIST

HMO investment financials

☐ Put together a personal financial statement (if not already completed in PART ONE)

☐ Discussed investment objectives with a financial advisor and assessed potential returns from property versus potential returns from other investments

☐ Sought out a specialist tax advisor and taken the time to really understand their advice

☐ Checked your credit score and taken steps to remedy any issues

☐ Fully considered key financial risk factors attached to HMO investments

☐ Put together an investment plan and clearly established how your investments will/ can be financed – work with your financial advisor on this

☐ Investigated with your IFA the implications of needing an HMO specific mortgage

☐ Read business administration books/guides and researched KPIs

☐ Become familiar with Excel, or a similar spreadsheet program

☐ Set up your own HMO viability spreadsheet (if not already done in PART TWO)

☐ Thought about the type of KPIs you'll need to track in YOUR business

PART FOUR:

HMO LEGAL ISSUES & LICENSING

Here, we look at the various legal considerations and issues involved in the purchasing of a buy to let property and the letting of it as an HMO – most of which you will not come across in buying your own home or a more straightforward single let investment property. The two key areas are planning and licensing, both of which are likely to apply to you as an HMO landlord. This part highlights your key obligations, outlining both the legal requirements and penalties for noncompliance.

Chapter 4 of 'HMO PROPERTY SUCCESS': The legals

Buying, owning and letting investment property is very different to buying and owning your own home and, especially in the case of HMOs, there are numerous legal considerations you need to become familiar with.

One of the challenges of being an HMO investor is keeping on top of and up to date with all the legal requirements associated with your investment, so you'll need outside help and advice on an on going basis. Some of this comes from engaging legal and financial professionals; some relies on you building relationships with local council departments and landlord associations; all of it demands that you, personally, understand the legal implications of every aspect of your property business.

Getting things right from the start will make life a lot easier and cheaper as you grow your portfolio. To many investors 'dip their toe in the water' at the start by buying one HMO to see if they fancy it as an investment strategy. They take very little advice before they make their first investment, on the basis that they can 'sort it out later', if they decide to press on. What they don't realise is that there are on going implications for the way some tax and legal matters are entered into and arranged at the outset.

Falling foul of your legal obligations can result in anything from a simple demand that you rectify a situation, to a criminal conviction, a hefty fine and prison time. In short, this is not an area you can afford to get wrong

Although I'm not a qualified legal expert, I do have a great deal of hands on experience as a 'consumer' in the field of HMO legals, so am going to highlight the key points I think you need to be aware of and regulations you need to comply with. I'm not going to go into a lot of detail because, a) I'm not a property lawyer, b) many of the precise legal requirements vary from council to council and, c) detail is what I pay experts for You can spend an awful lot of time getting bogged down in research into specialist areas that others have spent years training for, so save yourself the time and effort and engage those experts to advise you.

The legal set up and administration of your business

As I said in Chapter 1, it's important to speak to a wealth manager or independent financial advisor about your investment plans, so that they can look at property in the context of your other financial affairs. That will have an implication on the way you legally own your properties and structure your property business. Many buy to let investors own properties personally, then let and manage them through a Limited Company; some set up a new company, others use an existing one. For some people, having a company own a property portfolio is more suitable. Everyone's situation is different and you need to work with financial and legal advisors to decide on the right set up for you.

Having a Limited Company or Limited Liability Partnership brings its own associated legal requirements, including filing returns with Companies House and making declarations and filings with HMRC, and there can be heavy penalties for noncompliance. You will need to make sure your books are kept up to date and all legal and financial paperwork is filed properly.

Because HMO investing involves more certification, compliance and general paperwork than other types of property investment, I'd highly recommend you don't try to do it all yourself. I'll talk more about the team you should have around you later in the book, but three key members of that team should be:

1. A very good accountant who's a property tax expert
2. A legal representative with specific experience in buy to let investing
3. A bookkeeper experienced in buy to let – and preferably HMOs

You may be concerned with keeping costs down when you're starting out but, trust me, the cost of getting the right advice to make sure your business is correctly set up from the start is not a cost you should be cutting. Good professional advisors will end up saving you many times over what you pay them.

Conveyancing

Getting a good buy to let deal often relies on you being able to complete quickly, so your legal representative must be willing and able to move things along and look for solutions, not excuses Look for a legal/conveyancing firm that has experience specifically in the acquisition of properties for buy to let portfolios and try to make sure that the person dealing with your purchase is a buy to let investor themselves. They'll understand the things that are really important to you and know how to approach any problems that might come up.

As an HMO investor, it's more than likely you'll want – and usually need - to make alterations to the properties you buy, in order to make them fit for purpose. Extensions, movement or erection of walls and converting garages into bedrooms or living rooms are all very common, so whoever's carrying out your conveyancing needs to know these things are important to check in the property deeds and/or lease, in the case of leasehold properties. New build deeds often prohibit the conversion of garages and leases often state that you can't alter any internal walls, and if a conveyancer fails to highlight any such clauses to you, you could end up with a property you can't let in the way you planned - and that could be disastrous for your investment strategy.

Similarly, they need to know to particularly check for any previous planning applications/ issues and any upcoming changes in the law (such as the 'garden grabbing' legislation in 2010 that made it easier for local councils to refuse development requests) that might affect your plans for the property.

If you're buying with a spouse or business partner, you'll also need to decide whether to own the property as 'joint tenants' or 'tenants in common' for inheritance purposes (as joint tenants the property automatically passes to the other owner/s, whereas as tenants in common you can leave your share to any beneficiary in your Will). A good legal representative should be able to help you with regard to your Will and be willing and able to liaise with your wealth manager and mortgage broker to make sure you take ownership of the property in the right way, as quickly and efficiently as possible.

Planning

I don't think I'm over exaggerating when I say that planning can be a minefield. You need to be aware that your investment is likely to be subject to certain planning laws and those laws vary from council to council, not only with regard to building works, but also change of use. Ignoring the issue of planning is not an option.

National legislation currently states that you don't need planning permission to change a property's use class from C3 (standard single household home) to C4 (HMO of up to 6 people), BUT local councils can adopt an Article 4 Direction requiring that you DO apply for planning permission. The main issue with this is that the planning application process is likely to take longer than the conveyancing process, so you might end up completing on your purchase before a decision on whether to grant planning permission has been made.

You need to think very carefully about this, as entering into an investment that may turn out not to be fit for purpose could have serious financial implications for you. I've heard several horror stories about people who have bought properties without doing the necessary research – usually they've simply heard someone talk about the profitability of HMOs and have decided 'it doesn't sound that difficult to me…' – and they've ended up with a house in the wrong location that they can only let as a single unit, which doesn't cover their costs. They only have two choices: to let it out and keep subsidising the costs out of their own pockets, in the hope that the market will rise enough for them to sell and at least break even; or, to sell right away and take the financial hit.

The best you can do is talk to your local council planning department to find out what their policy is and approach your local landlords association to find out what other investors' experiences have been. There's also a lot of useful information on the Government's site: planningportal.gov.uk.

If you want your HMO to house more than six people, you will definitely need to gain planning permission, and I would always recommend you hire a local Chartered Town Planner to advise you and complete the application on your behalf. If you can build a good relationship with a planning expert, sometimes they're happy to give you a verbal idea as to whether a particular property would be likely to be granted planning permission (for change of use and also for any extensions or conversions you might want to carry out), although this would be in no way binding on their part.

Building regulations (an extension of Planning)

Another area where you need to make sure you're compliant. People sometimes make the mistake of thinking that if they're not actually 'building' anything – i.e. extending or converting lofts etc. – then building regulations don't concern them. They're wrong.

The main thing to know here is that if you're undertaking any work to the property, you must speak to the council about their building regulations policy BEFORE you start works, otherwise you can get in a mess, with regard to both their assessment and potentially having to redo work.

As well as having to comply with general building regulations, your HMO may need soundproofing. The planning department can advise you of this – usually it's only an issue with licensable HMOs – but it's not something you want to come as a surprise, because it can cost tens of thousands of pounds to sound proof a whole house.

Health & Safety

If your HMO is licensable, then the council will advise you of everything you need to do health and safety wise to make sure your licence is granted. But even if you don't need one, it's a really good idea – certainly on the first one or two properties you buy – to have someone from the housing department visit (Housing Standards Officer, or similar) to check you're doing things properly.

As a landlord, you have a legal duty of care to your tenants and must carry out a fire safety risk assessment, to show that you've identified and considered all potential risks and taken steps to mitigate them. You could do this yourself, but for around £200 a qualified Fire Risk Assessor will carry out the assessment for you and not only make sure you're doing everything legally required (such as ensuring your furnishings and furniture comply with fire regulations), but also make recommendations for additional sensible steps to take, for example, installing smoke detectors in all rooms (heat sensors in the kitchen) and fitting fire doors to all bedrooms and kitchens.

As far as how many of the 'additional recommendations' you should implement is concerned, a good rule of thumb is: are you satisfied that if anything happened to one of your tenants and you ended up in court, you could honestly say – and prove - you'd taken all reasonable steps to ensure their safety? That's why instructing a professional to carry out the risk assessment and going over and above the basic legal requirements are both advisable...I like to sleep at night

Certification required

HMOs, where tenants are sharing kitchens and bathrooms, don't currently legally need a valid Energy Performance Certificate (EPC), but I'm sure that will change in the future and so suggest you make one available to your tenants anyway.

What you absolutely DO need is:

1. An annual gas safety check, carried out by a Gas Safe registered engineer, and that record must be made available to the tenants (and copied to the local council if the property is licensed).
2. An Electrical Installation Condition Report certificate. All fixed electrical installations must be inspected and tested by a qualified electrician at least every five years and the local authority can require the certificate to be produced in 7 days – for any HMO, not just a licensed one.

As you've probably gathered, because so much of the legislation around HMOs is defined by local councils it's absolutely imperative you speak to the various departments individually (don't presume they speak to each other) to find out their overall attitude to HMOs and exactly where you stand with regard to:

- Planning
- Licensing
- Building regulations (including soundproofing)
- Electrical safety certification
- Fire safety (and speak to your local Fire Safety or Community Safety Officer)

Your local landlords association should also be a great source of information. I've found most other landlords are only too happy to share their experiences and steer you in the right direction.

The legal agreement between you and your house sharers

The document you should be using to form the legal contract between you and your tenants is an Assured Shorthold Tenancy Agreement (AST). In student properties, where it's usually a group of friends moving in together, it's common for there to be just one AST, which makes all the tenants jointly and severally liable for the total rent. But with HMOs for working adults, who usually don't know each other and don't want to assume responsibility for the rent in this way, landlords tend to issue separate ASTs for each room.

The key thing is that you understand and comply with your rights and responsibilities as a landlord. In simple terms, you are obliged to:

- Provide suitable, secure accommodation
- Properly maintain all fixtures, fittings and furnishings you've provided, in addition to the fabric of the property itself
- Ensure the health and safety of your tenants
- Allow your tenants peaceful occupation of the property
- Give adequate written notice to terminate the agreement

You can buy an AST 'off the shelf', from a stationers or online, but most landlords tend to want to customise it. DON'T simply do this yourself you could end up in a legal mess if any additional clauses were to be challenged, so always use a legal letting specialist to ensure that, a) the agreement is appropriate for letting to a tenant of an HMO and, b) all terms are legally enforceable. It's worth spending a few hundred pounds getting the contract right in the beginning, because you're going to be issuing a lot of them and need to be confident that your adapted AST will stand up in court.

Building regulations and planning

Most buy to let investors will try to find a property that is ready for tenants to move into straight away, to save time, money and hassle and ensure they receive rental income right from the start.

However, if building work is needed, the local council will insist the work is carried out according to building regulations.

These can vary and sometimes apply to even seemingly inconsequential changes to a property, so landlords must take expert advice before any building work is started. Not following the correct procedures can be costly and even result in work having to be reversed.

Visit your local council's website - gov.uk/find-your-local-council and find the contact details for their planning and housing departments. Different departments rarely speak to each other, so you may need to contact several different individuals.

Building work that must meet regulations includes:

- Installing a service, such as washing or sanitary facilities
- Material alterations to the structure
- Flat conversions
- Some major repairs, like replacing a roof

There are two main procedures relating to building works: full plans application and building notice procedure.

**Note that this is different to any planning permission you may need for change of use, as per Article 4 directions.

Full Plans Application

This is the standard procedure for most building works where the local authority's building control service will approve the plans before work starts. They can approve the proposals and may add conditions or make amendments.

Under this procedure a commencement notice is issued by the building control inspector when the work starts. At predetermined stages in the build, the contractor must call in the inspector to check on progress.

A completion certificate is issued at the end of the project to confirm that work was carried out according to the regulations.

Building Notice Procedure

This applies to small scale projects that need to be completed quickly and when pre approval of the plans is not essential.

The contractor gives a building notice to the building control service stating that work is about to commence.

The contractor will be notified if any of the work is not likely to meet the appropriate regulations so they can be amended as required. Inspections take place as the work progresses.

Housing Health and Safety Rating System (HHSRS)

The Housing Health and Safety Rating System (HHSRS) identify high risk premises for targeted improvement. It is a risk based evaluation tool that helps to protect against risks and health and safety hazards that may arise from deficiencies in a property. It was brought in under the Housing Act 2004 and applies to residential properties in England and Wales.

The HHSRS covers everything from sanitation and domestic hygiene to noise and reducing the risk of accidents.

Full guidance information can be found on the GOV.UK website online.

HMO licensing

Gaining planning permission to convert a property to an HMO is not the same as having a licence to run the property. The terms are not interchangeable and relate to different property issues.

HMO owners must apply for planning permission and a licence separately.

HMO laws talk about a 'property manager', who can be the HMO owner or someone appointed to run the home on behalf of the owner, including a letting agent. The manager holds the licence and must meet the 'fit and proper' person rules and make sure the property meets any legal or licensing conditions.

Licences last for five years and the cost varies between local authorities. Some councils give a discount if the landlord or property is accredited to a good landlord scheme or if the application is supported with a business plan.

Why HMOs are licensed

The key aims of a licence are to ensure that:

- The HMO manager is a 'fit and proper' person
- The property meets fire, health and safety standards
- The HMO is not overcrowded

Large HMOs are licensed because statistics show that people living in shared housing are more likely to live in poor conditions or face fire safety risks than the rest of the population.

By licensing, councils can make sure large HMOs are not overcrowded and meet strict safety regulations.

Small HMOs are a little different. Many argue that three or four students sharing a house cause no more issues than a family with a couple of teenage children living in a similar property.

Some councils choose to license small HMOs to curb issues like anti social behaviour by tenants. This covers a range of complaints, from noise to parking issues and overflowing rubbish. Another common complaint, especially in student cities, is that HMOs are overrunning family homes in some neighbourhoods, pushing down house prices and changing the demographic mix, which can have an adverse effect on services, like schools.

Who needs an HMO licence?

Owners of large HMOs do not really have a problem – they need planning and licensing.

For small HMOs, the situation is not so clear.

If a local authority has taken on article 4 direction powers, property owners need planning permission before opening a small HMO. Small HMOs of three or more floors will also be subject to mandatory licensing.

Councils can also mix and match article 4 directions with additional and selective licensing schemes.

(Review PART TWO: What is an HMO? for more on article 4 directions.)

For example, Oxford has a citywide licensing scheme for all HMOs, while Newham, East London, is the first council to require private landlords to register all rental homes in the borough – and there are 35,000 of them

For small HMOs, working out which rules apply is sometimes complicated. The best approach is to discuss HMO issues with the local authority before putting in an offer on a property.

HMO managers are responsible for applying for a licence, regardless of whether the council requests the application. Failure to license an HMO is an offence, which carries a penalty of up to £20,000.

If an HMO manager is convicted of operating a shared house without a licence, the tenants can apply to a rents tribunal for the return of up to 12 months' rent.

HMO licensing terms and conditions

Councils must grant an HMO licence to the property manager if the following conditions are met:

- The property is suitable for the designated number of tenants
- The licensee is the most appropriate person to hold the licence
- The proposals for managing the property meet council approval
- The manager is a 'fit and proper person'

The factors considered when deciding if someone is a 'fit and proper person' include:

- Convictions – for violent or sexual offences, drugs and fraud
- Track record as a landlord – especially any breaches of landlord/tenant law
- Discrimination – including any Equality Act convictions

If a landlord refuses to apply for a licence or cannot satisfy the 'fit and proper' person criteria, the local authority can step into manage the property.

Mandatory licensing

Mandatory licensing applies to HMOs that:

- Have three or more storeys
  and
- Are home to five or more people
  and
- Are made up of two or more households

Selective or additional licensing

Councils can designate neighbourhoods for selective or additional licensing, allowing them to set controls for small HMOs in those areas. These licences can come with specific conditions.

To apply this type of licensing, councils must show that:

- The area has problems because of poor HMO management
- Other actions to control the issue are not available
- The process is consistent with the local housing strategy
- Residents and landlords in the area have been asked for their opinions

HMO licence conditions

Mandatory and selective licences come with certain conditions and specifications. They will specify the maximum number of tenants allowed to live in the HMO.

General conditions include:

- A valid gas safety certificate
- Valid safety test certificates for electrical appliances
- Installation of smoke alarms and emergency lights
- A written licence to occupy or a tenancy agreement for each tenant

Councils can also apply other conditions, such as restrictions on use of the property and keeping the property in good repair.

Additional licensing schemes

The Housing Act 2004 gives local councils discretion to set up additional HMO licensing schemes.

These can cover smaller HMOs where management problems have been identified or other buy to let homes, but not HMOs covered by mandatory or additional licensing.

Additional licensing covers a designated area facing low housing demand or suffering from significant and persistent anti social behaviour.

If an HMO licence is not granted

If a property is overcrowded, not properly managed or the landlord is not considered a fit and proper person, then an HMO licence will not be granted.

The council must then make an interim management order (IMO) to take over the day to day running of the property. The IMO can last for a year or until other suitable management arrangements are made.

If this expires and no improvements are seen then a final management order (FMO) is issued and the council can take over the property for up to five years.

If the landlord or manager decides to stop operating a licensed HMO or reduces the number of tenants, then they can apply for a temporary exemption notice (TEN). This lasts for three months while the manager decides whether to apply for a licence, become subject to an IMO or cease to run a licensable property. A three month extension is also available.

Landlords have the right to apply to the Residential Property Tribunal Service (RPTS) within 28 days if the council refuses a licence, grants a licence with conditions, revokes or alters a licence.

Failing to apply for an HMO licence

A local authority can prosecute an HMO landlord who does not apply for a licence or allows more tenants to live in the HMO than the licence allows.

A fine of up to £20,000 may be imposed, and breaking any licence conditions can also result in fines of up to £5,000.Furthermore, if a licence is compulsory but a landlord does not have one in place, he will be unable to evict tenants under the notice only section 21 procedure.

Duties of HMO managers and tenants

Both HMO managers and tenants have legal obligations.

HMO manager duties

The HMO regulations put special burdens on the manager of a shared house. The manager should have a clear idea of their duties and responsibilities. These are laid out in the Management of Houses in Multiple Occupation (England) Regulations 2006.

Scotland and Wales generally follow similar rules, but regional assemblies have their own rules too. Breaking these regulations is a criminal offence and managers can be fined up to £5,000.

Some of the key duties of HMO managers are:

- Carrying out a fire risk assessment and taking action to minimise the risk of fire

- Ensuring all tenants have their name, address and contact number and that this information is displayed in a shared area of the house

- Keeping fire escape routes clear and providing working alarms, fire fighting equipment and emergency lighting. HMOs with five or more tenants must also have signs explaining what to do in case of fire.

- Ensuring gas supplies and appliances are tested once a year by a qualified professional and electrical fittings are tested every five years

- Making sure the common areas are clean, unobstructed and in good decorative order

- Taking reasonable steps to protect occupiers from injury because of the design or condition of the HMO

- Maintaining the water supply and drainage in proper working order to protect against contamination and frost

- Maintaining communal areas, fixtures, fittings and appliances in a clean, safe and working condition. This also applies to gardens, yards, fences and gates.

(See PART SIX: HMO safety, maintenance & repairs.)

HMO tenant obligations

The law places obligations on tenants and they can be prosecuted if they flout the law. They also risk losing their home. Some of their duties include:

- Letting the manager into their living space at reasonable times to carry out repairs.

- Avoiding causing careless damage to the property

- Disposing of rubbish as directed

- Complying with fire safety instructions

- Not obstructing the manager from performing his or her duties.

CHECKLIST

HMO legal issues and licensing

☐ Checked local council website for contact details: gov.uk/findyourlocalcouncil

    Housing Officer dealing with HMOs
    Name:
    Email:
    Phone number:

    Planning officer
    Name:
    Email:
    Phone number:

    Building regulations compliance
    Name:
    Email:
    Phone number:

☐ Understood Building Regulations procedure

    Notes:

☐ Checked and understood the Health & Safety Rating System (HHSRS)

☐ Ascertained local council's attitude to licensing and understood parameters

    Notes:

☐ Understood duties and responsibilities as an HMO landlord and manager

PART FIVE:

LOOKING FOR AN HMO PROPERTY

This part looks at the things you need to consider when sourcing suitable HMO properties, including location and type of property, budget and the routes through which you're most likely to find available stock. Much of the detail is covered in the book, in chapters 5, 7 and 8, so the additional content provided here serves more as a general guide and overview. Be sure to review all the checklists and information forms you have completed up to this point, as that information will form the framework of - and set the parameters for - your own specific property search.

REVIEW

By now you should be clear on:

- ☐ Why you're investing

- ☐ How HMO investing is going to satisfy your financial and lifestyle plans for the future

- ☐ Your target market – who you're intending to let to

- ☐ What you can afford

- ☐ Buy to let mortgages

- ☐ How to calculate yield and ROI and 'stack up' a property investment

- ☐ Your local council's planning requirements

- ☐ Your local council's licensing policy

If you can check all those points off and have completed each of the checklists at the end of each part, you're ready to move on.

Overview of property sourcing

Sourcing HMO properties often presents a real challenge. Finding the right size and type of property that can be configured well as an HMO, at the right price, in the right location can take some time.

And remember that the 'right' location may have nothing to do with general desirability because you're going to be focusing on areas where there is the highest demand specifically for rooms to rent. (See PART TWO, 'Types of HMO market'.)

Also, don't forget that this is a business acquisition, not an emotional purchase – you are simply looking for a property that satisfies the requirements in your business plan. A big garden might be a real draw for you, but will tenants really want to maintain it? The garden could end up as just one more job you have to manage and pay for.

Having already carefully assessed the needs of your target market, you should be well equipped to seek out the type of property that will suit both you and them.

If looking to rent to young professionals, a home close to a city centre, with good amenities and transport links is ideal. For students, the property should be close to campus and nightlife.

The area you are looking in may also dictate the type of house you buy - some suburbs have a higher prevalence of terraced houses; newer developments could be semi detached and detached homes.

Bear in mind that council housing departments have specifications for minimum bedroom sizes, so make sure you know what those are before you put in an offer or plan any alterations. An additional bedroom will not equal an extra rental income each month if it is too small to be usable. As long as you assess the size of the bedrooms to ensure that they offer a decent amount of private space for each tenant and make sure there is enough communal space if everyone is in the kitchen or living room at the same time, you should be able to present an attractive home to tenants.

Ultimately, what you want as a landlord is a property that is profitable and both easy to manage and attractive to tenants.

The key lies in looking at each property from two points of view:
1. that of a tenant, because you need to keep your rooms filled with satisfied people who are paying a decent amount of rent every month, and
2. your own, in terms of whether the potential profit gives a good return on the amount of capital you will have to invest.

Chapter 5 of 'HMO PROPERTY SUCCESS': Become your own local expert

As you're probably gathering, there aren't any short cuts to becoming a successful HMO investor – either financially or in terms of time and effort You'll get the best results from buying a property with built in equity that's in high demand – i.e. the right property, in the right location, at the right price – and doing that requires expertise.

While you can 'outsource' legal, financial, trades and management expertise, the best person to source property on an on going basis is you. You can tap into the knowledge and services of local estate and letting agents who know the area well, but they're highly unlikely to be experts in sourcing HMOs, so you're going to have to be able to quickly assess yourself what's going to work and what isn't.

Don't make the mistake of chasing after deals around the country, or let yourself be persuaded by investment companies and people selling leads that they've discovered the 'new hot spot' and can let you share in the good fortune of 'an incredible deal – but hurry, or you'll miss out…' Almost every town and city in the UK has a shortage of multi let accommodation and you can always find some kind of good deal locally, provided you know where and how to look, and how to negotiate.

Why doing it yourself is better than buying leads

Whoever's selling leads will tell you how well they know the area and how great their contacts are. They'll say they're either not in a position to buy the properties themselves or aren't interested in expanding their own portfolio any further, so are looking to gain some financial reward in another way: the fee they charge you for benefiting from their expertise.

The main issue with buying leads where you simply pay a fee is that the 'expert' selling to you has no on going interest in the property you buy. They get their fee whether or not you ultimately make money from the property, and when you're looking at investing as much capital as you are in an HMO, that's an awful lot of faith to be putting in someone else. I've come across far too many people who've bought leads that have turned out to be bad investments – at best, they just about break even; at worst, they're left with a property that's not worth what they paid for it and which nobody wants to rent at anything like a reasonable market rate. Yes, you can – and should – do your own research on any property you're considering buying, to satisfy yourself that it's a good deal and meets your objectives, but then what are you paying the sourcer for?

Look at how much they want to charge and work out how much of your own time that could buy – time you could spend getting to know your area really well – and you'll see that working on becoming your own local expert is a far better long term investment.

Why invest locally?

The question is, really, why not? If you happen to live in an area that doesn't have sufficient demand for HMOs (often the case with rural locations), you might need to look as far as an hour away, maybe more. But, as a rule, you will be able to find solid investment properties within easy striking distance – 15 to 30 minutes of your home.

Benefits of basing your portfolio locally:

1. **You can focus your efforts.** You can't possibly become an expert in all the various micro markets in the UK, so why not focus on a place you already know something about? By concentrating on just one area, you give yourself the best chance of success in that area.
2. **You can be where you need to be quickly.** Good deals often need acting on right away so there's a real advantage in being able to look at a property as soon as you hear about it and meet with vendors and agents. Even if you have someone else fully managing your portfolio, there will be times you'll want or need to visit your properties or deal in person with some issue, which is a lot easier – saving you time and expense when you're close by.
3. **It'll be easier to build good relationships.** You'll be on hand to liaise regularly with estate and letting agents, attend local property and networking events and can tap into existing contacts to find good trades people and suppliers Also, there's often a natural resistance to property investors from homeowners, but if you're a local yourself, you may find it easier to overcome that and also to negotiate with vendors.
4. **You can build your profile locally.** Become known for doing what you say you'll do and for running an ethical, reputable business. I have ***never*** shaken hands on a deal and then backed out, even when it's turned out not to be quite as good as I first believed. Your reputation is everything, so make sure people want to do business with you and talk about you for the right reasons. Get involved with local events and give back to your community, whether it's offering your time and expertise for free or helping financially, such as sponsoring a local sports team. Just make sure you do it for the right reasons and choose things that mean something to you – I'm talking about good PR, not shameless self promotion

"It takes many good deeds to build a good reputation and only one bad deed to lose it."
Benjamin Franklyn

And as your business and reputation grow, you'll find that other successful people will gravitate towards you and more and more opportunities will come your way – and not just in the property sphere. Through building my HMO portfolio I've been invited to lots of different business and social events and have now become a huge fan of motor racing and horseracing I've built friendships with people I've met at those events and have already partnered with several of them on different projects.

The expertise you'll need to gain

You need to immerse yourself in the property market so that you know exactly which properties, in which streets, at what price, will make good HMOs. And to make sure they're a good investment not only today but also into the future, you need to understand market trends and be able to spot local economic indicators.

The ability to value a property
Valuing a property is not an exact science – ultimately you can say that a property is only worth what someone will pay for it on a given day – but you need to get to the point where you have an instinctive feel for a fair price. You can only do that by building a bank of knowledge about what's recently been sold and looking at market trends, then putting that knowledge together with the current supply and demand situation: how much of what you're looking for is currently on the market and how many people are competing for that type of property?

You can find sold property prices online – **rightmove.co.uk** and **landregistry.gov.uk** are two of the best sources – but it's also worth spending time talking to estate agents. They'll be able to speak about specific areas with more knowledge, give you details of potential HMOs that have recently sold, and it's also a good way of testing which agents might be the best ones to try and work with going forward. You'll quickly see the ones that understand buy to let and are interested in building longer term relationships with investors/landlords.

A couple of good online tools for seeing what's currently happening to prices in your local area are:
- **mouseprice.com**, where you can put in a postcode and it will show you each property's marketing history: when it was listed, when and by how much it was reduced in price and when it went under offer.

- **the PropertyCBee toolbar** for Firefox, which will bring up all changes to the price and details made since the property was listed, for any property you look at on Rightmove and PrimeLocation, as well as a few other sites.

Using these tools, together with the information you get from agents, and your own additional research, should give you a very good idea of values.

Buying at the right price is so important for an investor. When it's your own home, you're often prepared to pay a little more than you really wanted to because of the emotional investment, but this is strictly business, so make sure you have 'number crunched' thoroughly and are as sure as you can be that the property will not only deliver the cash flow you need, but also be a good long term investment. Look at how average house prices in the region have performed over the past 20 years and then compare how the kind of properties you've identified as good potential HMOs have performed against that average. You should aim to buy property that has consistently outperformed or, at the very least, kept up with the local average, because that's a very good indicator that it will continue to do the same.

Recognising economic drivers

These are key to supply and demand in an area, affecting both the capital value of your investment and on going income potential. HMOs are most successful in areas where there are good transport links, decent local amenities, employment opportunities and a shortage of quality accommodation.

A lot of people simply look at what's going on in the area at the moment and whether it's 'regenerating', and that's a fair indication that there may be good current demand. But where's the investment coming from and what's the future plan? Wine bars and restaurants come and go; you need to know what the local plans are for the next 5/20 years, because you're in this business for the long term. You have to be as certain as you can that the demand for rooms isn't going to suddenly fall because either businesses are closing down in the area or a whole load of new multi let accommodation has suddenly been granted planning permission.

Information about future plans for the area is freely available from your local council, but you can usually get more in depth information from speaking to local businesspeople, other investors, good estate agents and surveyors who have lived and worked in the area for a while. And revisit this research every six months or so to make sure you're always aware of what's coming up and can adjust your investment (by changing how you let and who to, or selling and reinvesting in another property), if necessary.

The local council's attitude to HMOs.

Given that pretty much every council will have a slightly different policy and attitude towards HMOs, you need to become an expert in yours. You must know exactly where their boundaries fall, because neighbouring councils can have different regulations, for example, one might have adopted the Article 4 Direction requiring you to seek planning permission for any HMO, while the other might be happy for up to 6 people to share a house without planning. A common issue is parking. Some councils will only permit an HMO if there is a certain amount of off road parking with the property; others don't mind whether there is or not. Another consideration is how 'C3' they view an area, i.e. are there certain pockets that are considered 'family home friendly', where the council would refuse permission for a property to be rented out as an HMO? Depending on a council's attitude (and taking into account all your other research), you may decide not to invest in a certain ward if there are too many requirements and restrictions.

Tenant preferences

Different types of tenants often have certain areas, even particular streets that they like to live in, so you need to research where the kind of people you want to rent to are requesting rooms. Sites such as **spareroom.co.uk** and **uk.easyroommate.com** have 'wanted' adverts and you can usually see their employment status. Letting agents, even though they might not rent rooms out themselves, often know the particularly popular and not so popular areas. Working adults, for example, tend not to like living in a particularly student oriented area and want somewhere they can park, so narrower streets without off road parking, within walking distance of a university won't be suitable.

And find out what they're looking for, in particular. All house sharers prefer refurbished properties with decent kitchens and bathrooms and many expect wireless broadband, but what else does your target market expect – and are they happy to pay more for it? Is a cleaner expected, or satellite TV? You want to provide whatever there is a demand for, and a shortage of.

Rental values

While average property prices tend to peak and trough, rents are usually fairly consistent, so their performance over time isn't so relevant. What you need to focus on is how much tenants are prepared to pay for what level of accommodation. HMOs vary wildly in quality, so the average room rent for your area might actually be significantly lower than you could charge for what you're offering. Where I invest, double rooms vary between £350 and £500 a month.

As with the above, look online at what people are prepared to pay for an all inclusive room rent – SpareRoom puts out a monthly index of room rental prices, which you can access from the website for free - and then go and look at some of your competitors' properties. Get to know exactly what standard you need to provide so that you can charge the highest reasonable rent and still keep the property full.

You must also make sure you know the rental values for letting a property like yours as a single unit because, as I mentioned in Chapter 3, lenders may be basing their mortgage calculations on that single let value. An area might stack up well on purchase price and on going cash flow potential, but if it's an area that tends to attract low income families, the monthly rental value for letting the property as a family home might be too low to make the purchase worthwhile because of the amount of deposit you'd have to put in. Talk to local letting agents about your plans and ask their professional advice on which areas might be best to consider, then back it up with your own online research.

All the elements above combine to give you a detailed picture of the local HMO market. As you build your knowledge of values and analyse them together with costs and income to calculate potential returns, you'll start to see which areas/streets are most viable, with the right balance between accommodation potential, affordability, demand and capital growth potential.

There is no secret to success; it is the result of preparation
hard work and sheer determination.

Flats as HMOs?

As a rule, HMOs stack up best when they offer 5 or more bedrooms, so the vast majority are houses. However, in some areas a large flat or older converted property that you could convert back into single premises may present a good option. But there are some additional issues with flats:

The freeholder will have to give permission to sub let, so there must be a related clause in the lease or a written waiver that allows you to take in tenants. Such a clause may place restrictions on the number and type of tenants – for instance, many freeholders will bar students or tenants on benefits.

Flats may seem cheaper than houses, but once annual service charges, ground rents and maintenance fees are added in, the costs can mount.

One surprise to watch for is a block about to undergo extensive refurbishment, like painting the outside or replacing the roof. Each tenant's share of the cost, is determined by the floor area of their flat as a percentage of the total floor area of the block. So if you have one flat in a block of 10, you will have a bill of 10% of the cost, assuming all the flats are the same size.

And be aware that, because of the proximity of neighbours, you may have more complaints about noise, disturbance, etc. than you would with a detached house.

Location, location, location

The location of your HMO will have a huge effect on the number and type of tenants you attract and the rent you can charge. If you get the location wrong, you are likely to end up with an investment that doesn't meet your objectives and possibly a property that becomes a real liability. This is why your research into the demand in your area is so important. (Revisit PART TWO.)

People renting rooms want to live in a safe area, where they have shops, pubs and restaurants on their doorstep, and can get where they need to go quickly and easily, by public transport or car. Choosing a property in an area that covers all these bases will boost the appeal for tenants.

City centre locations generally bring higher rents, but many cities have undergone massive development in recent years, so tenants may have a lot of homes to choose from, especially in the new build apartment market. In these markets it's especially important to make sure demand is definitely there and likely to continue, and to look at whether any further development is planned for the area. Over supply of stock will result in rents falling and greatly increase the likelihood of void periods.

Corporate and professional lets are the most profitable options in major cities, but these tenants want value for money and will drive a hard bargain.

The suburbs are often a better option; just a mile or two outside a city can make all the difference. Here, properties are likely to be larger and more suited to four or more tenants. Provided there are good transport links and local services in the neighbourhood, and you have carried out your research properly, you should be able to acquire a property that will make a highly profitable HMO.

Take time to get to know the area you are considering and try to view from the tenant's perspective. Look into things like bus services, parking, crime rates and community organisations, so you can paint your property in a good light when talking to potential renters.

…and how close to you?

For some landlords, it is important that their properties are close enough for them to manage them directly. Others will be happy to let an agent handle the day to day business of viewings and maintenance and it will not matter whether they can get there quickly themselves.

Both options have pros and cons so weigh up how important it is for you to be directly involved in managing the property and how much it will cost you to get there if you live far away.

Your budget may limit your choice

Finally, your budget may well affect the areas where you can afford to buy property. Some cities or regions may be out of reach and you should be realistic when looking at what you can afford versus what you can expect to make.

In very high priced areas, such as central London, your research is likely to show that a larger HMO simply does not stack up in terms of purchase price versus rental income, and you won't get a very good return on your investment. In this case, a flat may prove a better option if you are looking for income. On the other hand, if you are simply looking to cover your costs in the short term and are more interested in capital appreciation, a larger property is likely to appreciate more than a smaller one.

In short, your investment goals will govern what you buy and where you buy it and if you are more interested in capital appreciation, then HMOs may not be the right vehicle for you. That's why it is so important you are clear on why you are investing and what returns you expect, when.

(Review PART THREE, 'Stacking up your investment'.)

Finding the right property

There are three main ways to track down your perfect rental property:

- Online
- Through an estate agent
- At auction

Each has pros and cons and different landlords will find that certain ways work better for them.

Online searches

There are thousands of websites advertising property for sale. Some are portals that aggregate properties offered by other websites and estate agents, while some are sites advertising homes for sale from a single company.

Always check more than one website and make sure you are registered with the two leading UK portals:

- Rightmove.co.uk
- Zoopla.co.uk

These sites cover around 90% of the properties for sale in the UK and are updated regularly as new houses come on to the market. You can set up alerts so that you get an email as soon as homes that meet your search criteria come online.

Estate agents

Estate agents work for sellers, so their sales patter should always be taken with a pinch of salt Do not let them pressure or persuade you into a property that is not suitable for your business. Their aim is to sell houses on their books, not necessarily to help you find the perfect rental property.

That said, those with experience can be extremely knowledgeable about the location and the market, offering you genuine insights that could help you make a decision.

As you carry out your local property research, you may find that certain agents carry more of the kind of stock you are focusing on, and it is worth taking the time to find the person/people within these agencies who particularly understand investing. Many professional investors end up using just two or three key agents, because they have built good relationships with them. An agent who really understands what you are looking for and why, can be a real help in your property search.

Always give clear feedback from viewings, explaining what is right and wrong about each property an agent shows you, to help them build a picture of your ideal investment.

Property auctions

Some landlords head to a property auction as they think they will be able to bag a bargain and save much needed cash. This occasionally happens, but is not the norm. One reason is that you may be bidding against people who are buying the property as their home, and when it's an emotional purchase, people tend to bid higher than makes good business sense. Secondly, the success of television programmes such as 'Homes Under the Hammer' has increased public awareness of auctions, so there are probably more people bidding than there would have been ten years ago.

Properties generally come to auction for one of two reasons: the house is in bad repair or it has been repossessed. Both of these situations can cause problems and alarm bells should already be sounding if a property cannot be sold through the usual channels.

Repossessed properties may be in poor condition and there could be a lot of work to undo boarded up windows and so on. Also, defective properties are often not mortgageable, which can cause financing problems.

Two key pointers for buying a property at auction:

- Check the property thoroughly before bidding. Look for structural problems with the advice of a builder, and potential issues with the title deeds with help from a lawyer

- Arrange finance in advance. A 10% deposit is often required when the hammer falls and if you cannot complete the purchase within 28 days, you could lose this money. A bridging loan can be used to secure the deal and the property can usually be remortgaged after refurbishment to get the money back.

Property sourcing firms

Property sourcing firms can take away some of the legwork of searching for a property and offer to find 'below market value' (BMV) properties as investment deals.

The firms work with homeowners who are desperate to sell and try to arrange sales around a quarter to a third below market value. A fee, which can be thousands of pounds, is then charged to the buyer for the sales lead. Sales are generally agreed privately.

Property sourcers come with a 'wealth warning' from the Office of Fair Trading, which is currently investigating whether some companies are offering fair deals to homeowners desperate to sell.

The indication is that this market may soon face regulation to root out the rogues. Don't forget, as property sourcing firms are not regulated, any money handed over is not protected if the deal goes wrong.

In short, be very wary about dealing with sourcing firms or individuals and ALWAYS make sure you get your own, independent valuation from a RICS surveyor to ensure you are buying at the right price. But if you have done your local area research properly and become an expert yourself, you really should not need to pay someone else for leads.

The property itself

Old v new homes

Victorian and Edwardian properties usually make great HMOs as the rooms are spacious with high ceilings and large windows. Newer developments do not tend to offer as much space but are preferable to some landlords and tenants as they are well insulated and usually need less maintenance.

The size and type of the house often impacts the amount of outdoor space too. Big gardens can be more trouble than they are worth, for both you and tenants, but older properties can offer better potential for off road parking, so this may be something of a trade off. If you have to employ a gardener, this will eat into your profits, while a simple yard is easy to maintain and still provides some outside space for tenants.

Properties with additional, secure storage space can also be a big draw. A basement or garage gives tenants somewhere to keep bicycles, sports equipment and suitcases. And that tends to come with older, rather than newer properties.

Size matters

When searching for a potential HMO property size really does matter. HMOs are for three or more people, so a house that allows for the conversion of living space into three or more good sized bedrooms is essential.

Think laterally. If the house has two or three bedrooms and two or more living rooms, you could convert one of the living rooms into an extra bedroom. And if there is an attached garage, you may be able to convert that into either a bedroom or a living room, depending on planning, covenant restrictions, etc.

Floor plans are very useful and most estate agents now tend to put them on the details, so you can take them home and 'play' with various different scenarios. Remember to ensure all rooms can be easily accessed from main hallways and landings and make sure you are clear on which walls are supporting structures.

The council will insist communal areas and shared facilities are adequate for the number of people living in the house. Common sense dictates that a property with more than four bedrooms should have at least two bathrooms, or at least one bedroom with an en suite, to reduce congestion.

Similarly, living rooms and kitchens must be large enough so that everyone can sit together if they so wish. Cramped living spaces and having to fight for the shower before work will not make your property attractive to tenants. The bedrooms should also be a decent size. Tenants will expect enough room for a double bed, wardrobe, drawers and a desk as a general rule.

Sacrificing space in order to squeeze in an extra single room may not make good financial sense. The additional rental income from that room may well be negated by having to lower the rest of the rents if there is less general space, and if there is an impression of cramped accommodation, you are likely to find the rooms harder to fill, which may result in void periods.

Putting your house in order

The condition of a property will have some bearing on the asking price, so investors can expect to pay more for houses that are ready for tenants to move into.

Properties that need work to bring them up to standard will cost less initially, but additional money is needed to fund refurbishment. Whether you opt for a perfect property or one in need of work will depend on your budget and how willing you are to spend time and money getting your house in order.

As a general rule, in HMO investing it's better to find a property in need of work, as you're likely to have to add or move bathrooms, refit kitchens and move or add internal walls in order to create the right internal space in any case, so it's simply not worth paying extra for something in perfect condition.

While it will mean you won't be able to move tenants in right away, the benefits of doing work yourself are:
- you should be able to tailor the internal space for your requirements
- the 'uplift' in the value of the property should certainly exceed the amount you

spend on the renovation/refurbishment
- provided you have a good team of tradesmen and/or can do some of the work yourself, it should present an enjoyable challenge

To help you decide the level of disrepair you are prepared to deal with in an investment property, consider:

- How long it will take to bring the house to a good state
- How much you have available to spend on the initial investment and additional repairs
- Whether you have the time and skills to manage the refurbishment project
- How much the work will increase the market price and potential rental yield of the property, and whether this is worth the time, money and effort involved.

With all these figures in mind you can fine tune your budget and tailor your searches accordingly.

(Revisit PART THREE: 'Stacking up' an HMO investment'.)

Chapter 7 of 'HMO PROPERTY SUCCESS':
Researching properties

The first thing you have to be clear on is who's going to rent your rooms and what they're looking for, because demand is the driver for your business. You can then start looking at the best way to satisfy that demand in a way that meets your financial objectives.

Your target market

I'd say that working adults between the ages of 20 and 35 will make up the vast majority of your tenants and they'll have all kinds of different requirements, depending on their job and personal situations. There might be a shortage of rooms in certain specific locations, for example, for NHS staff near a hospital or for commuting professionals close to a station, but, as a general rule, you need to cast your net wide and make sure your property appeals to as many people as possible.

General wants and needs of people renting rooms:
- A good sized double room
- Reliable shower
- Plenty of space in the kitchen
- On a bus / train / tram / tube route
- Easy walking distance to shops
- Parking
- Warmth
- Broadband

In certain, usually high-value areas in and around London, working professionals will expect an en-suite

Some of the things we tend to be very concerned about when we're looking for a home to buy such as a garden and sitting room – simply aren't that important when you're talking about an HMO. Fundamentally, people want a good private space and decent washing and cooking facilities; how well you satisfy the other requirements will make the difference between you letting your rooms more quickly than your competitors and being able to charge the top rents in the area. See Chapter 9 in PART SIX for more details.

Online research

These days you can find a huge amount of very up to date information about prices, room seekers and properties, quickly and easily online. You will need to talk to agents to get some more specific local information, but start with the internet so that you're well prepared for your discussions in person and can get used to analysing figures. The more online research you do, the better a feel you'll get for which properties in which areas would be worth viewing.

Tenant demand/s

You need to research what the demand *is* and what the demand is *for*. The top three sites I'd suggest you use are: spareroom.co.uk, easyroommate.com and gumtree.com. Go to the 'rooms wanted' section, put in your town or city name and see how many people are looking for rooms. Then do the same search for rooms advertised and if there are at least twice as many 'wanted' adverts as there are rooms available, it's worth taking your research further.

Go back to the 'rooms wanted' section and see which specific areas the people who are prepared to pay most want to live in. Again, put that area name or postcode into the 'rooms available' search and look at the supply/demand ratio. Once you've identified the areas where demand is outstripping supply by at least 100%, you can start to focus in on exactly what people are looking for, in terms of room size, communal facilities, parking/ bike storage and broadband/satellite TV, so you can start making a list of refurbishment requirements and associated budget.

Remember to use this research alongside your general area research for future demand. For instance, an area might have quite an average supply/demand balance at the moment, but if inward investment has already been allocated for transport or facilities, or businesses have confirmed plans to move into the area, they're strong indicators that buying into the area now could actually be a very good investment.

Property values

Rightmove.co.uk and landregistry.gov.uk are two of the most useful sites for checking past and current property values. You can search for properties by postcode and make comparisons over time, even breaking it down into types of housing stock (detached houses, semi detached houses, flats, etc.). The thing you won't usually be able to see is the condition of each property, but if you look at enough data, you should be able to get a pretty good idea of how much each type of property in each area is worth.

I'd suggest that you base most of your initial research on properties - in areas of high room rental demand that could provide a minimum of:

- 5 double bedrooms and one single
- Two bathrooms (one of which could be a shower room)
- A large kitchen/dining room or
- Good sized kitchen and a separate living room

Those are the basics of a fairly average HMO, which usually comes from reconfiguring / converting / extending a property that's currently being used as a family home. That might be something that:

- Already has all the required rooms if you simply reconfigure a current sitting room and dining room as bedrooms
- Offers the potential for conversion of a garage or conservatory into a bedroom or living area
- Has one or two large rooms that could be split into two – or more rooms

…hopefully you get the idea. Most of the properties that offer enough space will be detached or semi detached houses with three or four bedrooms, so start searching with those criteria.

You can easily spend several days looking at prices and comparing areas in terms of how much space you get for your money, which areas are holding their values well and which have suffered badly during the recession. Don't get too bogged down – all you need is to identify a reasonably accurate price range that you can use to work the investment viability numbers and an idea of which areas are likely to hold their capital values.

While you're looking at the property prices, also try to note how long properties have been on the market and by how much the original asking price has been reduced. As mentioned in Chapter 5, Propertysnake.co.uk tracks properties for sale nationwide and details when and by how much the property has been reduced, and the Property Bee toolbar for Firefox gives much the same information. This will help you build up an idea of the demand for each kind of property, as well as a realistic value, and also support your reasoning for future offers.

(And don't forget to check the rental values for letting this kind of property as a single unit, as that figure may be used by your lender in calculating your mortgage LTV amount.)

Narrowing it down…

You'll need to look at a lot of property details – probably over 100 - in order to end up with a shortlist of ten or so that are worth viewing. Most online details include a floor plan, which makes your life a lot easier, as you can quickly see whether the layout is going to work for you.

Once you find a potentially suitable property that's in the right location, at the right sort of value, you can really start number crunching, using different purchase price scenarios, maximum and minimum expected rental prices and approximate refurbishment costs. Your spreadsheet should be set up with formulae to auto calculate yield, ROI and profit so that you can easily compare the KPIs for each property. (This can and will be refined if you actually decide to proceed to offer, but for now you just need to know that it's financially worth pursuing.)

Armed with the printed details of the properties on your shortlist, you can now leave the house

Doing the legwork

Before you go and see any of the selling agents, have a drive past the properties, to get an impression of the location. Some things to consider:

If there are loads of 'room to rent' signs around, you may not have done your research properly

- If there are lots of 'for sale' boards, that's a sign supply is exceeding demand and you may be able to get a good deal on the price
- Look at the general state of the neighbourhood – does it appear relatively safe and reasonably well maintained?
- What's the parking situation?
- Are there any off putting things not mentioned on the online details, such as derelict buildings or electrical substations?

And do you like the look of the property? Although you're not going to be living in it yourself, you may need or want to sell at some point and you're certainly looking for something that will keep up with or exceed average capital values for the area. I always trust my gut when I look at a property and if I don't really like the look of it, regardless of what the figures say, I won't buy it.

Once you're happy with your drive bys, book viewings. If you've already met with the agents when you were doing your initial area/agent research, you can make telephone appointments, but if you haven't, make sure you go into the branch, introduce yourself and explain what you're doing. Ask the agents for their opinions on the properties you've shortlisted – including ones that are on with other agents and don't forget to check whether they have any new instructions that might be suitable, even if they haven't yet got hard copy details. You need to build an open, trusting relationship with the people who will probably be your main source of new acquisitions.

Viewing properties

When you're viewing a potential HMO for the first time, try to simply think of it as a box and don't get distracted by how it looks at the moment. Any wall that's not supporting can be removed; stud walls can be put up; garages and conservatories can be converted; bathrooms and kitchens can be refitted and/or new ones created. What you really need to look out for are the things that can add significant expense to a refurbishment project and/or that may make the property unsuitable, such as:

- Can all prospective bedrooms be easily accessed from communal areas?
- Are there any wall cracks wider than a 10p coin? That often indicates significant movement, possibly subsidence.
- Which side/end of the house is the plumbing currently on? Extending an existing plumbing system or installing a completely new one can be major works.
- Does the roof look in reasonable condition and is the chimney stack straight?
- Are many of the windows single glazed?
- Is there a connection to a telephone exchange?

Have a good look round outside, checking for anything you couldn't see when you did your drive by and look at any potential for building or extension – even if you're not planning anything at the moment, you might want to in the future.

A bit of advice for when you're looking at all this on your first visit is not to say too much about your plans to the vendor. Most of the properties you'll be looking at will be someone's home that they've loved and raised a family in, and the last thing they want to hear is that you're planning on ripping out walls and fixtures, painting over all their lovely décor and installing fire doors. Some vendors can get very offended and if they think you're only interested in how much profit you can make, it will only make negotiations harder down the line. Less is more in this case.

If you think you might be interested, have a brief chat to the vendor to find out their situation – why they're moving and their ideal timescale – as that'll give you an idea of whether it'll fit with your plans and, more importantly, how far you might be able to negotiate on the price.

Second viewing

If a property stood up to your initial financial analysis, you liked the look of it on the first viewing and it compares favourably with the other contenders, book a second viewing. When you call to book, confirm with the agent that you've understood the vendor's situation correctly and tell them you'd like to take your time on this viewing. Call your builder and ask if he'll go along with you to highlight any potential issues he sees and also recommend and estimate the cost of any works. If your builder isn't able to go with you, try to take someone else who can be a second pair of eyes – you can research approximate costs later.

Go through each room carefully and make a list of all the refurbishment work you'll need to do. If the vendor's there, ask them when the plumbing and heating systems were installed and last serviced and how old the electrics are. Essentially, by the time you leave this second viewing, you should have a very good idea of how much you're going to have to do to get the property ready to rent.

Detailed financial analysis This is the last step before you decide whether to make an offer and is really about confirming the price at which the deal stacks up for you.

Double check you've factored in all the refurbishment items and got realistic estimates/ costs for carrying out the work, then triple check you've included all the other costs associated with the purchase and getting the property ready to rent. Check the on going monthly cost estimates, work the numbers on an average income situation (although you should be confident you can achieve well above average income) and then also make sure you know what your 'break even' point would be as well as the maximum you can afford to pay.

You're almost ready to put together your offer…

Chapter 8 of 'HMO PROPERTY SUCCESS': Making an offer

Before you make an offer, you need to make sure everything's in place, ready to proceed, and that you put together your offer in such a way that it has the best chance of being accepted.

Take the details of the property or properties you're satisfied will make good investments, along with your financial analysis figures, to your broker. They won't be able to make any promises, but should be confident you'll be able to secure financing for the purchase. People talk about 'agreements in principle', but the reality is that until you put in a formal application and the mortgage valuation has been carried out, there's no cast iron guarantee that you'll get a mortgage. This is just one instance when you'll really see the benefit of having a specialist broker who has excellent relationships with lenders.

Instruct your solicitor (if you haven't already) and make sure you give them everything they need to be able to act for you – including documents that confirm your identity and any other instruction paperwork they require you to sign.

The other professional you'll need to source is a chartered surveyor who's accredited by the Royal Institution of Chartered Surveyors (RICS). Your mortgage lender will carry out a valuation, but you may need to instruct a Homebuyer's Report or Building Survey to get a more detailed report on the fabric of the property.

What should your offer be?

By now you'll have a very good idea of: a) what you think the property is really worth, b) the figure at which it works best for you without being a 'silly offer' and, c) how flexible the vendor is likely to be and now it's a case of juggling those things and putting together a reasonable offer.

Yes, every property has a value, but there's also a value to time. You need to be able to judge your vendor, understand their position and then negotiate a price that means you feel you have a good deal and so do they. If their time pressure is greater than their need to hold out for more money and you can help them move on without ripping them off, that's a win/win situation. Similarly, if the vendors want to wait until they've found somewhere to move on to and you decide you can work to a longer timescale that also has a value.

When you put forward your offer, it's best to do it in person, either to the vendor or to the agent:

- Explain why you're making the offer that you are (local research on sold prices, level at which your business model works, etc.)
- Confirm your position: that your broker and legal representative are ready to act for you
- Suggest a timescale
- Confirm everything in writing

If the offer is significantly lower than the asking price, you don't want the vendors to be offended, so do make it clear to them that you're basing your offer on the price that works business wise – you're not suggesting their home is vastly overpriced

And one very important piece of advice: be sure you're prepared to proceed with this purchase, because once your offer has been accepted – regardless of the fact that you're not under any legal obligation – you've made a verbal agreement. In my opinion, that morally obliges you to see the deal through (unless, of course, you get an adverse survey that significantly affects the property's value). I said it earlier: your reputation is everything and you certainly don't want to become known as someone who makes casual offers or pulls out of deals, especially in the area where you live and socialise.

WRITTEN OFFER EXAMPLE

(Available to download at nickfox.co.uk)

Dear <Estate Agent name>,

Further to our conversation, I am writing to confirm the offer I have put forward on <property address>.

As you are aware, this is an investment purchase. Having looked into the prices at which similar properties in the area have sold and the level of rental income I could expect to achieve, £<amount> is the price at which the property is a worthwhile investment for me.

My solicitor/conveyancer and mortgage broker (details below) have both been instructed and are able to act quickly. A mortgage has been agreed in principle, deposit funds are in place and can be accessed at short notice, and this purchase would not be dependent on any other property sale. Please feel free to contact my broker for confirmation.

If my offer is acceptable to the vendor, I will instruct a survey immediately and would like to aim for exchange of contracts as soon as possible, with completion <when>. *If the vendor has a related onward purchase, you should outline how flexible you are willing to be.

I appreciate my offer may be a little below what the vendors were hoping to achieve, but hope that my position is of some additional value to them.

I look forward to hearing from you.

Your sincerely,

Solicitor
<name, phone number(s), email   address>

Mortgage broker
<name, phone number(s), email   address>

If your offer's rejected...

...never go back to the agent immediately – take some time to reconsider the figures and your options. This is why it's a good idea to view ten properties initially: assuming you researched them properly before viewing, you should end up with two or three you'd be happy to proceed on. Always know your limit and be prepared to walk away from a deal if it gets too expensive or the vendors get too vague on the timescale. Your investment business plan will be based on a certain number of acquisitions a year and it's rare that you're able to be completely flexible on completion dates.

The first thing to consider is whether you're prepared to increase your offer. If so, you might choose to make it conditional, such as offering X amount more, provided completion takes place on or before X date.

If you're not prepared to pay any more, then explain why not and say you'll leave the offer on the table for a certain length of time (I usually give them a week), in case the vendor decides to reconsider.

If your offer's accepted...

Have a small celebration Then you'll need to be like the conductor of an orchestra for the next few months, making sure your ducks stay in line.

Get things moving with your mortgage broker, who will make sure the lender instructs the valuation as soon as possible, and have your solicitor confirm to you that they've agreed the timescale with the vendor's solicitor. Most solicitors will be resistant to agreeing exchange and completion dates at such an early stage in the process, which is why you need to work with a buy to let specialist who understands the importance of keeping your plans on track. It's also worth checking out whether you can gain access to the property to start refurbishment work before completion. Most of the time this won't be possible, but there are exceptions and it's worth asking, as every day the property is untenanted, you're funding the mortgage repayment yourself.

You may think the property is completely sound, especially if you've had your builder give it the once over, but for the sake of around £500, I'd rather instruct a Building Survey and find out about any hidden problems before my refurbishment team find them or – even worse – serious problems emerge once the property's tenanted.

You also need to meet with your project manager, go through the refurbishment plan (see the next chapter) and ask him to make sure his team will be available to start as soon as the purchase completes.

Speak to your local council planning department about your plans for refurbishing the property so you can make sure you're compliant with building regulations before work starts (your project manager may do this for you). Also, if you've been told you don't need either planning permission or a licence to let this property as an HMO, ask them to confirm it in writing. If you do need to apply for either one, then make sure you do that as soon as possible.

Complete, sign and return all paperwork you receive from your broker and legal representative right away and make sure deposit funds and fee and disbursement payments are all where they're supposed to be in good time. Although the estate agent (or their sales progression department) will be contacting your legal representative for updates on a regular basis, it's a good idea to speak to them yourself every now and then. Ideally, liaise with the vendor directly, so you can reassure them that everything's going smoothly and arrange any extra visits to the property you might need.

And, importantly, speak to a buy to let landlord insurance specialist – your mortgage broker will probably have a recommendation – to make sure you'll have the right insurance in place not only when you take ownership of the property, but when your tenants move in.

While every purchase is different and the timescales can vary wildly, depending on the vendor's position and your own situation, you should expect the process, from offer to completion, to take around three months. Your conveyancer will be able to provide you with information about each step involved – familiarize yourself with it so that you can not only make sure you're doing everything you need to, but also know where the other parties involved should be with their paperwork.

PURCHASE PROCESS
(Available to download at nickfox.co.uk)

This is an outline of the usual financial and legal process involved in a property transaction. All good solicitors/conveyancers and mortgage brokers should progress your purchase efficiently, but you should understand yourself how it works, so that you can ask all those involved the right questions at the right time.

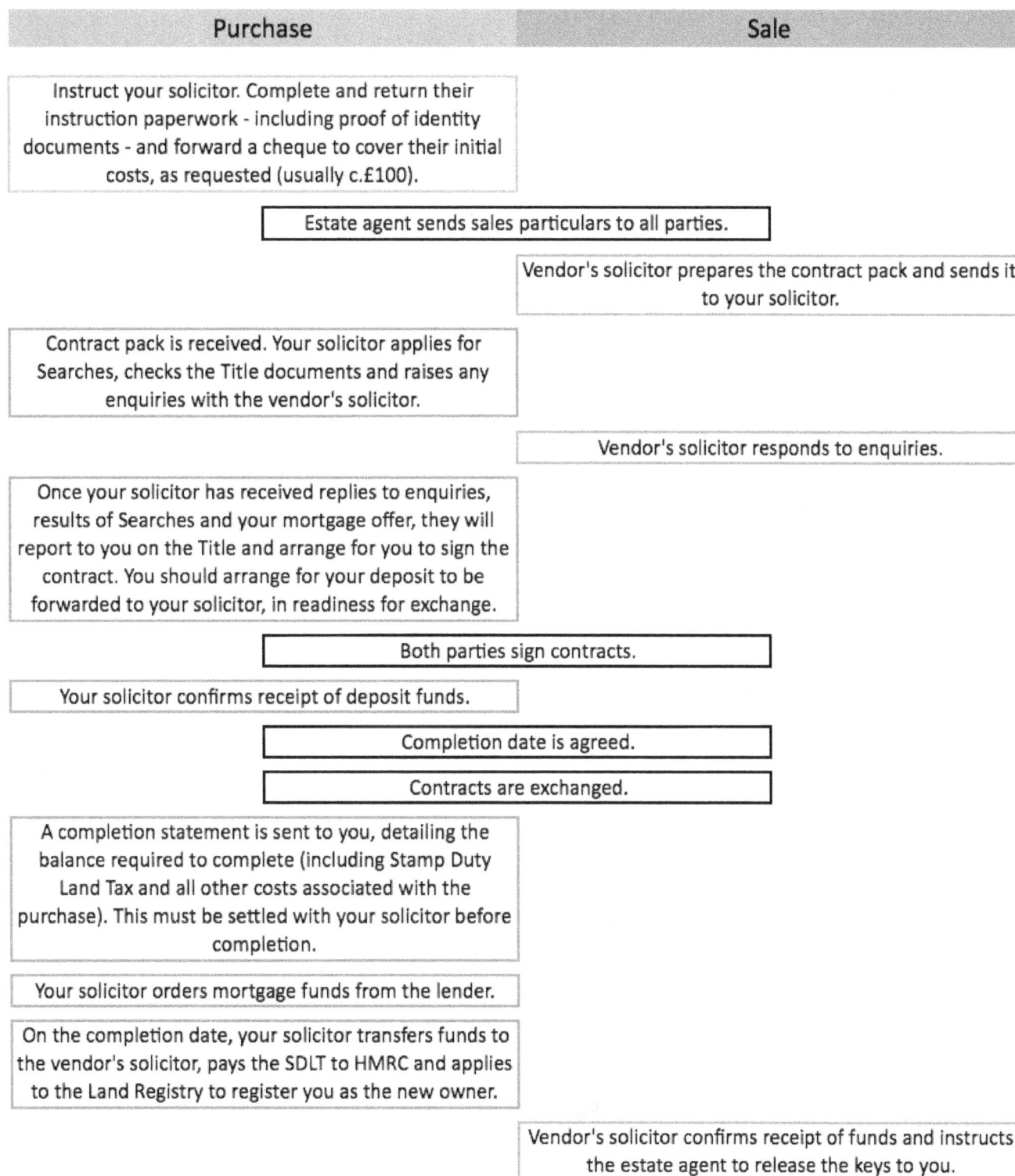

Purchase	Sale
Instruct your solicitor. Complete and return their instruction paperwork - including proof of identity documents - and forward a cheque to cover their initial costs, as requested (usually c.£100).	

Estate agent sends sales particulars to all parties.	

	Vendor's solicitor prepares the contract pack and sends it to your solicitor.

Contract pack is received. Your solicitor applies for Searches, checks the Title documents and raises any enquiries with the vendor's solicitor.	

	Vendor's solicitor responds to enquiries.

Once your solicitor has received replies to enquiries, results of Searches and your mortgage offer, they will report to you on the Title and arrange for you to sign the contract. You should arrange for your deposit to be forwarded to your solicitor, in readiness for exchange.	

Both parties sign contracts.	

Your solicitor confirms receipt of deposit funds.	

Completion date is agreed.	

Contracts are exchanged.	

A completion statement is sent to you, detailing the balance required to complete (including Stamp Duty Land Tax and all other costs associated with the purchase). This must be settled with your solicitor before completion.	

Your solicitor orders mortgage funds from the lender.	

On the completion date, your solicitor transfers funds to the vendor's solicitor, pays the SDLT to HMRC and applies to the Land Registry to register you as the new owner.	

	Vendor's solicitor confirms receipt of funds and instructs the estate agent to release the keys to you.

CHECKLIST

Looking for an HMO property

Making sure the property stacks up

☐ Researched sold price data on rightmove.co.uk and landregistry.gov.uk

☐ Looked at how 'for sale' prices are currently shifting, via propertysnake.co.uk and Property Bee

☐ Compared the performance of 'HMO type' properties with the market average over the last 20 years

☐ Spoken to local agents about the current local market and trends

☐ Researched rental values for letting both rooms and the property as a single unit

☐ Looked at the rental index data on spareroom.co.uk/rentalindex

☐ Confirmed specific tenant demand: exactly what do they want, and where?

☐ Been to visit existing HMOs for competitor research

☐ Tested purchase and rental figures on an HMO viability spreadsheet

Making an offer

☐ Confirmed 'power team'

☐ Put together offer in writing

☐ Understood and prepared for purchase process

PART SIX:

GETTING READY TO LET

After finding and buying the perfect rental property, the hard work continues Part six takes you through all the formalities of preparing the property to be legally let. It covers the steps you must take to ensure you, your business and your property comply with all the legal requirements, including: gaining permission to let, health & safety, insurance, Council Tax, furnishing and the pros and cons of letting and managing yourself versus using an agent.

Refurbishment

Every property purchase will require a different degree of renovation and refurbishment. Chapter 9 of HMO PROPERTY SUCCESS takes you through the key considerations and methods to ensure successful completion of your project.

Chapter 9 of 'HMO PROPERTY SUCCESS':
Refurbishment

Assuming everything goes smoothly with the purchase, you should be able to collect the keys around lunchtime on day of completion. You now need to do everything you can to get paying tenants happily settled in their rooms as soon as possible and that relies on meticulous planning. If you plan well and there are no unforeseen delays, I'd say you should be able to complete a fairly comprehensive refurbishment (gutting, updating plumbing and electrics, refitting bathrooms and kitchen, then decorating) in around four to six weeks.

Before you do anything else, go and introduce yourself to the neighbours and let them know that there will be work going on for roughly the next 4 weeks (or however long). Reassure them about what you're doing and give them your contact details so they can get in touch if they have any issues or concerns. Again, this business is all about relationships and taking the initiative in this way will be much appreciated.

Your refurbishment plan

Meet your project manager and his/her team on site to confirm exactly what needs to be done, map out floor plans and agree an achievable timescale. Ask them to supply written quotes and you might want to put together some kind of incentive scheme – perhaps that you withhold a percentage of the invoice until you're satisfied there aren't any 'snagging' issues after completion of the project or a bonus for bringing it in on time and to standard.

All the contractors you engage MUST have the correct liability insurance and they should also be suitably accredited and/or members of relevant trade associations or bodies (see Chapter 6).

You then need to sit down and create a detailed written plan (I find a spreadsheet is best) that includes:

- Every job required, broken down by room
- The contractor required for each job
- A schedule of works, showing the length of time each job will take
- All health and safety elements

- Dates and times of deliveries of supplies/materials from external suppliers/contractors, e.g. carpet fitter
- Dates/stages when you'll need to adjust your insurance, depending on when the property's furnished and occupied

Go through it carefully with your project manager to make sure you haven't missed anything and that he/she's also happy the team can work to the final schedule.

It takes a fair amount of work the first time you put one together, but if you take time to get it right, you'll have a great template for all future projects. I share mine on a cloud based system so that everyone involved in the project can see exactly what stage we're at and I liaise regularly with my project manager in case any of the plans need revising as we go along. Also remember to update your financial analysis spreadsheet if any of the refurbishment costs change.

Health & Safety

Before you start any renovation or refurbishment, you must make sure your planned work is going to comply with Building Regulations. You should already have checked this out with the local council; if you haven't, then don't start any works until you have, or there may be penalties.

Then, even though you may be happy that you understand your health and safety responsibilities, it's a good idea to ask the local council Housing Standards Officer and Community Safety Adviser (or similar from the Fire Service) to come to the property while you're refurbishing it. You can explain to them exactly what you're doing and make sure they're happy with your plans. You don't have to pay for this and it avoids you having to possibly make changes at a later date. Particular points to query with them are:

Housing Standards Officer
- Are the kitchen (particularly cooking) facilities suitable for the number of people?
- Are the room sizes acceptable (especially important if you're creating new rooms by putting up stud walls)?
- Are the proposed bathroom facilities sufficient?
- Are there any other facilities I should provide that I've missed?
- Community Safety Adviser
- Is the fire alarm system (or smoke detectors) I'm intending to install acceptable?
- Do I need to put up fire exit signs?
- Are the fire escapes (which can simply be ground floor windows that open wide

enough and at the right height) acceptable?

- Where do I need fire doors?
- What fire safety equipment do I need in the kitchen? (usually extinguisher and blanket)
- Do I need any other fire extinguishers?
- What lock systems do I need on fire escape routes? (Your front door/s must be able to be opened from the inside without a key)

In terms of fire regulations, even if you're not licensable, it's sensible to ask a professional for their opinion on what's a reasonable level of safety.

Personally, I choose to err on the side of caution with health and safety. As I said earlier in the book, you have a duty of care to the people living in your HMO and need to take all reasonable steps to ensure they don't come to any harm.

Ask both the Housing Standards Officer and Community Safety Adviser if they'll come back once the refurbishment is complete and confirm their findings in writing. They may not – sometimes verbal advice is all they're prepared to give – but you should also ask one of them if they'd be happy to go through the fire risk assessment form for you. Again, they may not, but it's something that a suitably qualified professional should carry out, as they're better placed than you are to assess levels of risk. You may have to pay a Fire Risk Assessor to complete it for you, which can cost anywhere between £100 and £300 – not a great deal, in the grand scheme of things – and you can easily find a local assessor online.

Security options for room doors vary greatly, from Yale locks to code entry panels; you can also get keys that can be suited, to reduce the number of different keys you and/ or your property manager have to hold. It's entirely up to you, but bear in mind that tenants will occasionally lose keys, lock themselves out and sometimes move out of the property without returning their keys, so you need to be able to gain entry and resecure the property easily. Ask around at your local landlords association and see what other people find works best, but if you do use keys, particularly for the main front door, I'd recommend you pick a system that gives you full control over who can duplicate them.

'Interior design'

This is where you need to strike the right balance between finish and budget. Your décor, fixtures, fittings and furnishings need to be hard wearing, modern and visually appealing, while staying within budget. An average of six people coming and going all the time means that, no matter how well you start out, your property is going to suffer quite a high level of wear and tear, so make sure carpets don't show dirt and stains easily, pick paint colours that will always be readily available, so that walls and paintwork will be easy to touch up, and make sure the kitchen and bathrooms are easy to keep clean. Most of this is common sense

It's impossible to be prescriptive on cost, but I'd suggest you shouldn't spend more than £600 on furnishing each bedroom and make sure the furniture you buy for the communal areas is built to last…on the understanding that you'll probably have to replace most items every five years or so.

In terms of where you get the furniture from, it's a bit like finding good local contractors – there'll be somewhere in your area that deals in low cost, sturdy furnishings, so ask around your team and other landlords. I have a great supplier, who now knows exactly what I need and can kit out whole houses for me as well as replace individual pieces of furniture very quickly.

Minimum furnishing requirements:

Bedrooms:	Bed with mattress, wardrobe, drawers, curtain/blind
Living room:	Sofa/s and/or chairs (seating for at least 4 people), table, television DVD player
Kitchen/utility:	Large fridge (6 shelves min), large freezer (6 drawers min), good sized oven and hob, washing machine, adequate drying facilities (either a coin operated tumble dryer or space for drying racks). Some landlords also install a dishwasher, but it's not essential.

You then need to stock the kitchen with everything you'd expect to find there (crockery, cutlery, glassware, cookware, utensils, kettle, toaster, microwave, etc.) and have an iron, ironing board and vacuum cleaner stored somewhere in the property. Essentially, all the tenants should need to provide for themselves is bedding and towels.

Finishing off and getting 'ready to rent'

Once the property is completely refurbished and furnished:

- Make sure your gas & electric checks have been carried out and display the certificates in the property – the kitchen is usually the best place
- Have the Fire Risk Assessment carried out by a suitably qualified professional and take any recommended steps
- Install wireless broadband, making sure there's sufficient bandwidth allowance to handle six people online at the same time

- Get the property thoroughly cleaned and arrange for an on going cleaning service to take care of the communal areas – I'd suggest at least once a week
- Have a pin board in the hallway or other communal area that clearly displays:
  - fire escape information
  - the property manager's information
  - what to do / who to call in case of an emergency
  - refuse & recycling calendar
  - issue log, for your manager to see
- Make sure you have enough keys cut. As well as supplying the tenants with keys for the front door(s) and their rooms, if necessary, both you and your property manager should hold a full set and you're likely to need additional copies of at least the front door(s) for your cleaner and handyman, plus a set to give out to contractors.
- Ensure you've documented everything that's been done and carefully filed all your receipts, as a lot of the work may be tax deductible
- Go back to the neighbours to let them know that work's finished and thank them for their patience

Then stand back and see what finishing touches you need. Put up a few pictures in the communal areas and also a couple of mirrors, which can really lighten up a dark hallway or landing. Remember that the doors to the bedrooms will be shut all the time and, particularly downstairs, where you've used what used to be reception rooms, that can make the house quite gloomy. A mirror will reflect what light there is and add a bit of depth to narrower areas.

And, lastly, while it's still looking brand new and perfect, try to choose a sunny day and take as many pictures as you can to use in your advertising – at least one of each room, including the bathrooms. More and more landlords are also making video 'tours' of their properties, so, if you can, do that as well. Take a few props to the house (bedding, lamps, plants, flowers, fruit bowls, etc.) to make it look homely and make sure you get all the shots you need, because once tenants have moved in, it'll never look quite like that again

At the same time as refurbishment is taking place (if not before), landlords must prepare for the lettings process, understand their licensing obligations and decide whether to work with a letting agent.

The regulations do change from time to time, so if you are unsure or want to double check where you stand on a certain issue, always speak to the local authority or lawyer before acting.

Permission to let

Landlords with a mortgage against their HMO must make sure the lender is aware that the property will be rented out as a multi let. This may sound obvious, but not everyone buys a shared house on an HMO specific mortgage and buy to let mortgages generally have clauses forbidding house sharing, demanding a single tenancy let.

Similarly, if you have a residential mortgage on your own home and either decide to take in lodgers or move out and switch the use to an HMO, the lender will have to give permission to let.

Don't forget that you will also need specialist buildings insurance. Standard home insurance will not cover a buy to let, HMO or a home taking in lodgers.

Leasehold permission to let

Leaseholders almost always have a clause in the agreement that prohibits sub letting.

Landlords who are not freeholders of the property must apply in writing for permission to let the property. The freeholder cannot refuse a reasonable request, but may limit the number of tenants and specify how complaints regarding noise, parking and rubbish must be handled.

Without these permissions from lenders and freeholders, landlords face repercussions, such as eviction and withdrawal of mortgage financing.

HMO safety, maintenance and repairs

More than 100 different laws place obligations on landlords who rent out homes.

Some are old and rarely acted on, while others are more strictly enforced.

Many of these legal requirements are dealt with under HMO licences (see PART FOUR) and tenancy/licence agreements. (Covered in PART SEVEN: Marketing & letting your rooms.)

As a blanket rule, a rented home must be maintained by the landlord and tenants to the standard that existed on the day the tenancy started, allowing for fair wear and tear. The responsibilities of each will be outlined in the rental agreement.

Gas and electrical safety

One of the most important responsibilities that landlords have is ensuring the safety of all gas and electric installations and appliances, which must be inspected at least once a year by a Gas Safe registered engineer. A copy of the certificate must be given to tenants.

Find a Gas Safe engineer in your area at gassaferegister.co.uk.

There is no legal obligation to check the electrical installation in shared houses, but landlords do have a duty of care to make sure that appliances and fittings are safe and it is recommended that a Electrical Installation Condition Report is commissioned at least once every five years. Annual Portable Appliance testing (PAT) is also recommended. Councils can stipulate that electric inspections are carried out each year as part of HMO licence conditions.

Visit the Electrical Safety Council website at esc.org.uk for more information on condition reports. You can find out more about PAT at the Health & Safety Executive website – hse.gov.uk – and locate a qualified PAT electrician via niceic.co.uk.

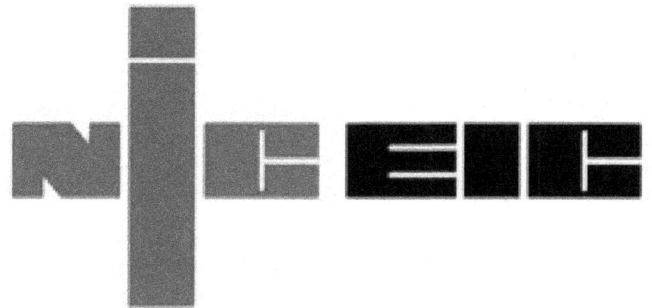

Energy Performance Certificate (EPC)

Every rental property should have a valid Energy Performance Certificate (EPC). This details the energy rating of the home, giving tenants an indication of energy efficiency.

An EPC is valid for 10 years and landlords must have an EPC in place before they market a property.

Furniture and soft furnishings safety

If an HMO is let furnished, all furniture must meet fire safety regulations, as set out in The Furniture and Furnishings (Fire) (Safety) Regulations 1988. Sofas, beds, mattresses and other relevant furniture should have a fire safety label in order for the property to be legally let.

The regulations apply to all furniture and soft furnishings, including cushions, pillows and seat covers. Linen, curtains and carpets are exempt.

RESISTANT

If tenants bring in their own furniture or furnishings, then the landlord is not responsible for their fire safety requirements.

Looking after the property

Landlords have a duty to keep the inside and outside of a rented home in a good state of repair, including:

- Gas and electrical fittings
- Maintaining the structure of the building
- Looking after fittings, like showers, sinks and kitchen units
- Servicing and repairing heating and hot water systems
- Cleaning and looking after shared common areas

Tenants also have certain duties when it comes to repairs and maintenance.

- They should not carry out any work unless it is specifically stated in their tenancy agreement, with out prior written permission from the landlord

- Tenants should take care of the property and put right any damage that is not fair wear and tear. Wear and tear covers things such as scrapes and scuffs incurred in the course of everyday living, but any items provided by the landlord that are broken or missing should be repaired or replaced.

Right of quiet enjoyment

Tenants have the right to live in their home without unreasonable disturbance from the landlord, letting agent or anyone acting on the landlord's behalf, i.e. except in an emergency, landlords should not enter the property unannounced. At least 24 hours' notice should be given if anyone needs to come into the property for repairs, maintenance or viewings, etc.

The full rights and responsibilities of landlords and tenants will be set out in the tenancy agreement. (See PART SEVEN.)

HMO insurance for landlords

Specialist landlord insurance is provided by a number of different companies and several types of insurance are available as standalone or bundled policies for HMO landlords.

Besides the standard building and contents insurance, public liability cover is a must and you may want to consider additional policies.

Buildings insurance

Landlord building insurance is usually a condition of any mortgage offer. This provides cover for the property in the case of damage caused by things such as storms, fire and subsidence.

Accidental damage is included as standard in some policies and as an added benefit costing extra in others, so you must check exactly what is covered.

Be aware that a buildings insurance policy will not cover general wear and tear, for example, if the windows or fascias are rotten, that's not an insurance issue.

If the property is leasehold, the freeholder is responsible for insuring the building. The leaseholder generally pays a share towards the cost in the service charge.

It is vital you check that you have the right cover before buying, by fully disclosing the details of any rental property, otherwise insurers may void the policy in event of a claim and keep any premiums paid.

Contents insurance

Landlords should take out contents insurance for carpets, curtains and white goods, etc.

Tenants should have their own cover for personal contents they bring into the property, as they are not included under the landlord's policy.

Liability insurance

Liability insurance is a must. It pays out if either a tenant or visitors to the property - such as contractors, the postman and tenants' guests – make a claim for personal injury suffered due to a fault with the property.

The insurance covers legal costs, compensations costs and expenses related to the claim. Standard cover comes as multiples of £1 million.

If the HMO has sole or joint owners, and they have no liability cover, the cost of claim is their personal liability and can put their own homes and other property assets at risk if they have to settle a large compensation claim.

Rent guarantee insurance

Also known as rent guarantee cover, this takes care of legal expenses and a rent if a tenant falls into arrears and refuses to leave the property. The risk of arrears can vary depending on the type of tenants sharing the HMO. Tenants on housing benefits and working singles present the highest risk, but all private lettings do a certain element of risk.

The cover can include legal fees in case an eviction is necessary.

It is likely to be a condition of the policy that a credit reference is performed on each tenant before they move into the property and any deposit is protected in line with current legislation. If these criteria are not fulfilled, rent guarantee cover is unlikely to pay out.

Emergency repair cover

This will cover plumbing, electrical and gas incidents, but remember it's a call out to fix the problem, not to provide a permanent repair and the cost of a tradesman needs adding on top.

Some insurance policies have this included as standard. If it is not included, you can buy standalone cover or add emergency repairs to the policy as a 'paid for add on'.

Portfolio insurance

Some specialist landlord insurers offer portfolio cover, which offers discounts for landlords who place more than one property on the same policy.

Empty buy to let insurance trap

Unoccupied homes may not have landlord insurance cover.

Many insurers consider a home unoccupied when no one has lived there for 30 consecutive days.

This means that if you are facing long void periods, you must check your insurance documents and ask for amendments from the provider, if necessary. Some insurers expect landlords to drain water systems if the property is empty for long periods over winter, and services may need to be shut off at the mains.

The rule also covers homes under refurbishment. Builders or other visitors to the property do not count as occupancy.

You are likely to need one kind of insurance while refurbishment is taking place, another once the property is furnished and then the appropriate cover once tenants move in. If you are in any doubt, or there is a change in the status of the occupancy of your property, contact your insurer to ensure you always have the appropriate level of cover.

HMOs and Council Tax

Council Tax is complicated to work out and depends on the number of people living in a home, their age and whether they are 'counted' as people liable to pay the tax.

If an HMO has a mix of counted and uncounted tenants, the property may still have a Council Tax bill, although other discounts and exemptions may apply.

Tenants on benefits may receive an extra allowance if their share of Council Tax is collected with the rent.

In any case, you should check with your local council and ensure the property is correctly registered with them.

Who doesn't count for Council Tax?

These people who are common HMO tenants are included in the list of those not counting as adults for Council Tax purposes:

- People on apprentice schemes
- Full time college and university students
- People under 25 who are funded by the Skills Funding Agency or Young People's Learning Agency
- Student nurses
- Foreign language assistants registered with the British Council

Full time students

HMOs let to full time students are exempt from Council Tax. To count as a full time student, the course must:

- Last at least one academic year
- Involve at least 21 hours' study each week

If a tenant is studying for a qualification up to that of A level and is under 20, the course must:

- Last at least 3 months
- Involve at least 12 hours' study each week

Empty properties

Landlords still have to pay Council Tax on empty and unfurnished homes, but may qualify for a discount. The local authority can decide whether you get a discount and how much you get, so you will need to talk this over with their Council Tax department.

Letting furnished or unfurnished?

This is not generally an issue for HMO landlords, as tenants want to move into a home that is ready to use.

Most HMOs are similar to hostels, where the tenants just bring in their bedding and personal belongings, so you should plan to let the property furnished, while leaving some scope for the tenants to make their living space personal, for example, with pictures and the odd small piece of furniture.

Keep the flooring, walls and furnishings neutral, to give the best impression of light and space. Tenants can then add colour with wall art, cushions and throws, etc.

Flooring should be fit for purpose and hard wearing. Be aware that the leases on many modern apartment blocks ban laminate floors in order to minimize noise for neighbours.

Kitchens should have white goods – fridges, freezers, a microwave, cookers and a washing machine – and enough crockery and cutlery for the tenants and visitors.

Most students and younger tenants have a stack of electronic gadgets that need to plug in for charging, so make sure rooms have plenty of sensibly placed sockets.

Freeview TV and broadband should be installed to the main living area and accessible from each room, but recoup the cost in the rent. Some landlords choose to install Sky, but, given the options for streaming online these days, that may be an expense you can avoid; instead, make sure there is adequate download capability on the broadband for the number of tenants. If you have fibre optic in your area, that shouldn't be a problem, but if you have standard broadband, you may need to acquire a booster or look into bonded ADSL. If you have advertised the property as having broadband, you need to make sure it is fully available as it's a key issue for many tenants.

You should also look to provide secure storage for bikes, suitcases and large items like sports gear, either within the property, or outside in a large shed or garage.

Laundry is another key issue, so if you can provide a well ventilated room or specific area where tenants can dry their clothes, that will minimize surface mould accumulating in their individual rooms and avoid them attempting to dry their laundry in the communal areas.

Managing an HMO

One of the most important HMO management decisions for a landlord is whether to take the job on or hand over the day to day running to a letting agent.

Sometimes the decision is a given – for instance, if the property is a considerable travelling distance from the landlord's home.

Before making a decision, go through a mental checklist of all the tasks involved in letting and managing an HMO and really think about whether you are able and happy to deal with all of it yourself:

- Marketing the property and finding tenants
- Dealing with rental agreements and deposits
- Moving in tenants
- Managing the property and looking after safety checks and repairs
- Collecting rent and managing financial records
- Dealing with problem tenants
- Checking tenants out

This work can add up to a lot of extra hours for landlords, particularly if they have a portfolio of several properties, and it may prove hard to juggle with another job or planning family time. Professional investors do not tend to go into the business to spend their time dealing with lettings administration, so go back to your goals and reasons for investing and calculate whether it is better to pay to outsource. You will probably find it is

Self managing an HMO

The list above is by no means exhaustive and checking tenants out is not the end of the job, but just the start, as the cycle of marketing and finding new tenants starts again.

One of the problems most landlords find most onerous is dealing with emergency calls from tenants.

Good customer service demands that a telephone or email hotline is always available to receive complaints and that they should be actioned as soon as possible. This can eat into a landlord's time and disrupt personal engagements. Of course, the calls and tasks multiply by the number of tenants in an HMO and the size of a portfolio.

This is one good reason many HMO landlords hand the job of property management over to a letting agent or private portfolio manager.

And even when the phone is quiet and the property seems to be running smoothly, the behind the scenes tasks involved with running any business still need looking after. HM Revenue and Customs expect landlords to keep good financial records as well as any other trader and, assuming you are approaching this with the intention of building a significant portfolio, you will need to ensure you employ people you can rely on to administer your property business on your behalf.

Multitasking is just one of the talents a self managing HMO owner needs – along with DIY skills, an ability to communicate with tenants and knowing how to effectively organise time and budgets.

Using the services of a letting agent

If you opt to place the HMO with a letting agent, you will probably be offered three levels of service:
- Tenant finding
- Let - rent collection
- Full HMO management

Tenant finding

A tenant finding service is something of a middle ground between self managing a property and using an agent for full management.

For a fixed fee, the agent will handle the marketing of the HMO, arrange viewings and get references and credit checks on potential tenants. The cost will vary between agents, but should be somewhere between 5% and 10%.

Once the tenants have moved in, the landlord then deals with any day today management of the HMO.

An agent may also offer a rent collection service, where they are responsible for ensuing the tenants pay the rent to them, then they pass it on to you. Again, fees will vary.

Full management

New landlords and those with demanding jobs or family commitments would probably be better off taking a fully managed option and can expect to pay up to 20% of the rental income, plus VAT.

Although that might sound a lot, it does include everything, from sourcing tenants to looking after the on going maintenance of the property for you, namely:

- Marketing the HMO and screening/referencing potential tenants
- Checking in tenants and taking an inventory
- Collecting and protecting deposits
- Collecting the rent
- Handling inquiries and repair requests
- Arranging maintenance work from reliable professionals
- Regular property inspections
- Help with HMO licensing issues and safety certificates

Choosing the right letting agent

Don't choose a letting agent based on cost. The cheapest is rarely the best.

If you can, seek out some references from other buy to let or HMO landlords in the area and search Google for online comments and feedback.

Ask the letting agent some key questions:

- Do they belong to an industry regulatory body? If not, why not?

- If they have no regulation, then you have no recourse to an independent industry body or the property ombudsman to arbitrate complaints

- Do they have a client money protection scheme? (If they do not belong to a regulatory body, then the answer is probably no.) Steer clear of any letting agent without a client money protection scheme, as they can simply close up shop and disappear with your cash.

- How many HMOs do they manage, what type of tenants do they have and where are they located? Not all letting agents handle HMOs. You want to know your agent has experience in this specialist area, has prospective tenants on the books looking for a home and covers the neighbourhood where your HMO is located.

- What is their occupancy rate / void average?

Once you are satisfied the letting agent can handle your property, start discussing costs and see if you can negotiate a portfolio discount if you have more than one property, even if the others are single unit buy to lets.

Assessing letting agents

This may come as a surprise, but not all letting agents are honest and above board in their dealings.

Even if their web sites and paperwork display logos from industry regulators, always contact the regulator directly to check that they are still members. Some unscrupulous letting agents have been known to join a body and then resign once they have a membership number. They then continue using the number and logos to seemingly add professional status to their business.

The main lettings industry regulatory bodies and organizations are:

Association of Residential Letting Agents (ARLA)
arla.co.uk

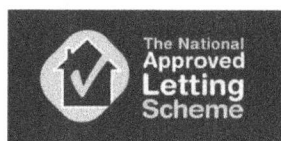

The National Approved Letting Scheme
(NALS)   nalscheme.co.uk

The Royal Institution of Chartered Surveyors (RICS)
rics.org/uk

The Property Ombudsman
tpos.co.uk

SafeAgent
safeagents.co.uk

Always use an agent that is a member of at least one professional body.

Keeping time with the academic year

Timing your HMO purchase and preparations for letting with the academic year is important if your target market is students.

Students will want to move into their home in September, and will generally stay until May or June. Some will want a full 12 month tenancy but many may only want the agreement to cover the academic year. This gives landlords a clear timeframe for purchasing and making ready a property.

However, bear in mind that students for the academic year starting in September will want to get their accommodation sorted before the end of the previous term, so viewings will need to take place by May at the latest.

While students will doubtless appreciate you offering a tenancy that matches the academic year, this could leave you without rental income over the summer period. You could offer short term contracts to foreign language students, in the UK for just a few months over this period, or – ideally – insist that students sign up to a full year's agreement.

Either way, if you are letting to students, make sure you check with the local university for the dates of any housing fairs.

Telling the tax man about your HMO

If you are starting a property business, you must tell HMRC that you have a new income stream within three months of the date of first letting. Once you've done that, you do not then have to tell them every time you add a new property to your portfolio.

Your letting tax year

The 'date of first letting' is the official start date of a property business and coincides with the start date of the first tenancy agreement or licence to occupy.

The tax year runs from April 6 to the following April 5, but the first year for your purposes will run from the date of first letting until the next April 5.

So, if you bought a property in May 2014 and the first tenant moved in on September 20, 2014, the first tax year runs from September 20, 2014 until April 5, 2015.

The next is from April 6, 2015 until April 5, 2016 and so on, until the business stops trading.

If the business ceases trading on June 30, 2018, the final tax year runs from April 6, 2018 until June 30, 2018.

Landlord accreditation

Joining a landlord accreditation scheme is not mandatory, but signing up will help to give potential tenants confidence that you are a fair and reliable landlord.

Accreditation schemes allow landlords to show that their properties comply with the relevant safety and legal standards and are managed properly.

Some HMO licences come with the condition that landlords attend a course on running a rental property and these may highlight the benefits of belonging to an accreditation scheme.

Under the schemes, either the landlord or the property is accredited. To gain this status, landlords may have to attend a course and pass a test and/or the property must pass a stiff inspection.

All proper accreditation schemes must meet some key values:

- The declaration – A voluntary declaration by the landlord or manager to meet set processes and standards

- Verification – The scheme must verify that those signed up are meeting the required letting standards set by the university, landlord body or local authority running the scheme

- Continuing improvement – Accepting that there is always room for improvement

- Complaints – A simple, inclusive, transparent and rapid complaints procedure must be in place.

Local council accreditation schemes

Many local authorities run accreditation schemes for landlords. Accreditation comes with some perks, such as discounted insurance and tenant referrals from councils and universities, so is certainly worth pursuing.

The exact details and requirements vary between councils and, as the accreditation is reassessed at intervals, the status may be withdrawn if standards fall.

The separate London scheme run by borough councils are about to join into a single London wide scheme, with landlords porting current membership into the new set up.

Joining a local authority scheme is voluntary. Landlords have to demonstrate:

- They are a 'fit and proper' person to manage an HMO
- The property is in good condition and meets safety and legal standards
- Management practices are fair and reasonable
- Community relations are maintained, such as managing waste, noise and parking

National Landlords Association (NLA) accreditation

The NLA runs an accreditation scheme for private landlords, which is based solely on landlord development and good property management. The scheme offers consistent standards that landlords, tenants and local authorities recognise and can rely on.

To become accredited, landlords must:

- Attend a foundation course
- Complete an online course
- Join the scheme through a regional landlord association

Membership often qualifies members to HMO licence discounts from local authorities.

The Unipol code (student homes only)

The Unipol code sets specific standards for shared student homes and how they are managed. The code covers properties with up to 14 tenants and is valid right across the UK.

Landlords and managing agents can join the scheme voluntarily to demonstrate their commitment to maintaining standards. Unipol accreditation aids students in choosing a suitable home and assures them standards and management meet a minimum quality.

CHECKLIST

Getting ready to let

Preparation for refurbishment

- ☐ Permission to let secured (if required)

- ☐ Licensing secured (if required)

- ☐ Planning permission secured (if required)

- ☐ Compliance with Building Regulations established

- ☐ Informed neighbours about planned work / timescale

- ☐ Got written quotes from contractors

- ☐ Appointed a Project Manager

- ☐ Agreed an incentive / bonus scheme

- ☐ Created a detailed refurbishment plan

Health & Safety

- ☐ Met with Housing Standards Officer at the property

- ☐ Met with Community Safety Advisor from the fire service at the property

- ☐ Carried out Fire Risk Assessment

- ☐ Got all certification required

  - ° Gas safety

  - ° Electrical installation condition report

  - ° EPC

- ☐ Chosen key system

Decorating & furnishing

- ☐ Planned a neutral décor

- ☐ Found hard wearing fixtures / fittings supplier/s

- ☐ Found a good local furniture supplier

Finishing off refurbishment

- ☐ Installed wireless broadband

- ☐ Found cost effective energy supplier/s

- ☐ Had the property thoroughly cleaned

- ☐ Clearly displayed house, safety and local information for tenants

- ☐ Cut enough keys

- ☐ Put in 'finishing touches'

- ☐ Taken photos (and video)

Other

- ☐ Registered for Council Tax

- ☐ Got the correct insurance

- ☐ Researched letting agents for management (if not self managing)

- ☐ Informed HMRC about the property

- ☐ Looked into local council accreditation schemes

PART SEVEN:

MARKETING & LETTING YOUR ROOMS

Here, we follow on from the preparation steps covered in the last part, looking at what you need to do to effectively market your property, tenant referencing, the legal agreement between you and your tenant, taking and protecting deposits and moving tenants in.

Marketing an HMO

All that hard work you have done to find and prepare your HMO for tenants can now come to fruition.

There is a lot of administration involved in marketing and letting your rooms – including preparing tenancy agreements and inventories, and keeping good financial and legal records – so you must be sure you either have the skills to do that yourself, or engage the services of someone else who can. That might be an agent or a private lettings manager, but this part should give you a very good guide for how to do everything yourself.

Finding the right tenants

Sourcing tenants depends on your target market.

Most people look for homes to rent through web sites or smart phone apps. If you are with a letting agent to find tenants, then this will be set up as part of the service.

If you are a DIY landlord, some web sites will offer properties to let for you.

Accredited landlords may find that they do not have to spend too much time and effort looking for tenants as the schemes help promote them to people looking for accommodation. But even so, making some steps towards finding tenants could speed things along.

Here are some typical marketing options for HMO landlords:

METHOD	PROS	CONS	SUCCESS RATE
Flyers	Cheap	Time consuming, hit-rate is very low	Low
Newspaper ads	Quick and easy	Many local papers have seen circulation fall	Low
Accreditation/university schemes	Can cut out some of the work	Not all tenants start their search by looking at accreditation schemes	High
Signs outside properties/Adverts in local shops	Seen by people in the area – but students are not locals	Not all tenants are already in the area they want to move to	Low
Internet	Most student and professional tenants start their search online, cheap	Email alerts let you know when tenants make a property inquiry	High

Advertising an HMO to prospective tenants

Advertising starts with attracting the attention of prospective tenants with attractive inside and outside shots of the HMO, which you should post online, along with a detailed description of what facilities the property offers, the benefits to tenants of the location and exactly what is included in the monthly rent.

Look at other rooms currently advertised on SpareRoom and Easyroommate, etc., to see how other landlords are advertising and make sure yours is up to standard. You might want to consider a premium listing, particularly if it's a 'sticky' time of year, so you can be sure prospective tenants see your property in the first page of search results.

Posting a video tour online helps attract viewers as well. Start on the street outside and go through the HMO room by room in a logical sequence.

Prepare for taking photographs / videos by tidying the garden, moving unsightly bins and rubbish, and 'dressing' the inside of the property, with bedding, cushions and plants, so that it looks homely and clean. Make sure the property is well lit and that you really are presenting it in the best possible condition.

Your marketing could start before any refurbishment is completed. Although you won't be able to take nice photographs, many tenants are attracted by the idea of being the first to move into a freshly updated property. Just make sure the site is safe enough to conduct viewings.

Conducting & managing viewings

If the property is empty, visits can be booked whenever is suitable for the prospective tenant. However, if there is already a tenant in the room being re let, you MUST give them notice before entering the property. (See PART SIX: Right of quiet enjoyment for tenants.)

Once marketing has begun, you must have an organised way of booking and keeping track of viewings, including written notes of who you meet and when, and your impressions of each prospective tenant. If you have chosen to engage a lettings agent, they will already have systems in place.

Keep a checklist and ask each viewer the same questions – including contact and financial details, so if you have a list of prospective tenants, you have some way of grading them. Note down:

- Name, email address and best contact number
- Time and date of their call
- Their current address and whether it's a rented property
- Their job status
- Are they claiming housing benefits?
- How they found out about the property / useful for your market research
- Time and date for viewing, and do they need directions?
- Do they have a car and will they need parking?
- Can they offer a guarantor who owns their own property?

If you can co ordinate several viewers at one time, you could hold an 'open day'. Opening up the property for a few hours is more time efficient than showing several people round individually, in separate appointments. Saturdays are the best open days, but consider an open evening for those that work at weekends.

If your prospective tenant is arriving by car, make sure there is somewhere for them to park.

Outside, make sure the area around the front door is rubbish free, swept and clean – and that includes wiping down white UPVC doors and windows.

Inside, have the lights on and doors open and, if it's chilly, put the heating on. Make sure the property is clean, especially the kitchens, toilets and bathrooms, and that everything works – some viewers will flush the loos and turn on taps and showers.

Have copies of safety certificates, the EPC, liability insurance and licences available, as well as a copy of your tenancy agreement, in case tenants ask to see them.

A guided tour may not be practical if you have a lot of viewers, so you might want to provide an information sheet with key details such as rent, breaking down what is included and any extra services.

For out of towners, some information about the local area will be of interest. For example, students might want to know the walking distance or travelling times to campus.

During the viewing, gauge people's feelings about the property. If they highlight any negative points, you can then address these to improve its appeal.

If you have more than one HMO, make sure you cross market if one is full or not quite suitable for someone. You could also consider moving them initially into a temporary room and transferring them to their preferred property as a room becomes available.

Review: Chapter 10 of 'HMO PROPERTY SUCCESS':

Part one: Getting tenants into your rooms

This is only a short section, because it's really not that complicated. There's the advertising and then the viewings and, provided your advert is good and you 'vet' your enquiries properly, it shouldn't take very long to fill your rooms, particularly when the property is newly refurbished.

One bit of advice I'd particularly highlight is that there's no reason why you can't start marketing the property while the refurbishment is still going on. Obviously, wait until the walls have been plastered and there aren't wires dangling everywhere, so that it's completely safe, but taking enquiries a week or so before you're actually ready to rent can sometimes mean you already have tenants ready to move in on the day the work's finished. The downside is that you won't be able to post any internal photos on the advert, but don't underestimate the attraction of the prospect of fresh paint and a brand new boiler

Where to advertise

The vast majority of your target audience - young professionals - will certainly be searching online on SpareRoom, EasyRoommate and Gumtree. It's not cheap to keep adverts running and well promoted, so while you're starting out, I'd suggest only advertising on one of those sites and doing it properly. Go back to your research and see if one site shows a greater demand than the other, in terms of 'room wanted' adverts for your area, but SpareRoom is probably the best option currently. Put up as many pictures as you can and, if you've been able to take video footage, put that up as well. The more of your property prospective tenants can see in the advertising, the more likely they are to feel positive about viewing.

You might decide to also try the local newspaper, but that can be quite expensive, so make sure you carefully track how many enquiries you get and the quality of them, to see if it's really worthwhile continuing. I've certainly found that I get a high number of unsuitable tenants calling from newspaper adverts – unemployed, on benefits or with a child – and it wastes time having to deal with these enquiries.

If you have a hospital close by, see if the HR department will take your details and put an advert up on their intranet. Sometimes larger businesses will also do this, but they may only work with you if you are a locally accredited landlord. If you haven't done so already, look into accreditation schemes and see if you can enrol.

Handling enquiries

When you're first starting out, it's important to track where your enquiries are coming from, how many turn into viewings and how many of those turn into lets. You need to know which adverts are generating the right quality of responses so that you can focus on those in future.

Make sure you always take a full name and number, ask where they saw the advert, establish that they're in employment and find out when they need a room and for how long. You can then offer to show them the property.

'Selling' your rooms

You're not just marketing the property when you conduct a viewing as a landlord; you're marketing yourself. I've heard of people deciding not to take a room, not because there was anything wrong with the accommodation, but because they were put off by how the landlord behaved with them, so be aware of how you're coming across

If they're keen to take one of the rooms and you're happy to accept them, you can then confirm the date they'd like it and the price, take a holding fee and make arrangements with them for moving in. Sometimes the first person to view a room will take it, but I'd say, on average, you need to conduct three viewings to secure a tenant.

What I would say is: trust your gut. If, while you're showing someone around, you feel unsure about them – for any reason – then don't hesitate to put hem off. The last thing you need is a troublesome tenant who either doesn't get on with the other house sharers or stops paying rent, so don't feel bad about turning them down. Never accept a tenant you're not sure about, just because you want to fill the room – another tenant will come along soon enough.

Selecting & referencing tenants

Once someone has expressed an interest in renting a room, they should complete a rental application form.

This will ensure you have standard, comparable information to hand to decide which tenants to take on. Groups of sharers should complete a form for each individual, even if they are signing one AST with a lead tenant, so you have everyone's individual details in case of any problems.

As well as personal and contact details, ask for:
- Permission for a credit check
- Proof of identity - like a driving licence, passport or bank statement
- Guarantor details

Avoiding discrimination

Landlords may have their opinions about the tenants they like or dislike, but discrimination laws apply to property owners as much as owners of any other kind of business.

You must not give anyone grounds for accusing you of discrimination by refusing their application for accommodation without good reason. If in doubt, take the application and consult a specialist lettings legal professional before rejecting them.

Many landlords do not allow smoking in the property, favour professionals over tenants claiming benefits or ban pets. Nevertheless, landlords must not break the Equality Act 2010, which states no one can discriminate against another person on grounds of:

- Race
- Colour
- Gender
- Religion
- Marital status
- Disability

Anyone who lets property commits an offence if they discriminate against a tenant on these grounds by:

- Refusing to let to them
- Setting unfair terms of rental

- Dealing unfairly with a list of people who need a particular type of property
- Refusing to provide access to benefits or facilities to a tenant
- Evicting or harassing a tenant

Anyone who is approached for consent to let or sub let a property and fails to grant consent on any of the above grounds also commits an offence.

For example, the Equality Commission explains that a private landlord who advertises a 'flat to let to Christian families only' could be discriminating on the grounds of religion or belief. In this case, both the landlord and the person publishing the advertisement could be liable to legal action.

Credit checks

Credit checks should be carried out on all tenants and guarantors – especially if the landlord has rent guarantee insurance. (See PART SIX: Rent guarantee insurance.)

The credit search gives a snapshot of the tenant's financial history. The information includes information about bankruptcy and court judgments for bad debts, as well as details about borrowing and whether payments have been made on time.

A poor credit history two or three years ago does not necessarily make someone a financial risk, but a trend of regularly missing payments and collecting court judgments for bad debts is a warning sign and landlords would be ill advised to rent a room to someone with that kind of financial history.

There are a number of credit referencing agencies/companies that you can find on the internet, but your local landlords association should be able to advise you of which one(s) their members tend to use.

Requesting a guarantor

Young tenants, especially students, are likely to have trouble providing references and credit histories, as they may not have rented before or taken out any kind of credit or loans.

Ask for a guarantor for the rent but make sure you also credit reference the person vouching for the tenant and verify their identity, just as you would if they were the ones renting from you. Ensure they own a property so they are traceable and you have something against which you could secure a judgment in court.

Telling a tenant they can move in

Once the decision to let is made, notify the tenant that they can move in and set a date for the tenancy agreement to start.

Before the tenant moves any property into the HMO or is given the keys, all tenancy agreements should be signed, a deposit taken and the first month's rent paid in advance.

Taking a holding fee

Asking a tenant to pay a holding fee gives landlords reassurance that the tenant intends to move in and demonstrates their financial commitment. It is advisable that you do not stop marketing the room until you have received this payment.

A holding fee is a non refundable application fee that covers the costs of setting up a new tenancy. It should cover the cost of credit searches and any fees for drawing up tenancy agreements.

Be aware that this is NOT a tenancy deposit and therefore does not need protection.

Agreeing the rent

The rent must be agreed with a tenant before any documents are signed.

This agreement includes not only how much is to be charged each week or month, but also the payment date and method of payment. If rent is collected weekly, then tenants must have a rent book, by law. Cash payments should be receipted, with a copy signed and kept by both tenant and landlord. Most landlords ask for rent to be paid electronically directly into their bank account. This ensures that both sides have proof of when payment was sent and is by far the most advisable method.

The tenancy agreement

Tenancy agreements are legally binding documents and can be complex, particularly for first time landlords. They outline the rights and responsibilities of both landlord and tenant, protect the interests of both parties and can help avoid disputes.

The most popular residential tenancy arrangements are the assured shorthold tenancy (AST) and a licence to occupy. Different rules govern each. Landlords who are unsure of which type of agreement to use should seek legal advice, as each agreement gives a tenant different rights.

A tenancy agreement:

- Gives the tenant possession of all or part of a property
- Calls for the tenant to pay rent
- Lasts for a fixed or periodic term

Without exclusive possession of the property, the tenant is a licensee.

Landlords should not allow a tenant to move in until they have signed a tenancy agreement or licence to occupy.

Some key issues regarding tenancy agreements:

- Landlords cannot insist tenants sign an agreement after they have moved in
- Without a valid tenancy agreement in place, evicting tenants is a problem
- Tenants without a written agreement have a legal right to ask for a written statements of the main terms, such as the date the tenancy began and the rent amount
- Tenancies can be created by oral agreement, although should always be written so that there is a hard copy record of what was agreed between landlord and tenant
- Anyone with exclusive occupation and paying rent is regarded by the courts as a tenant
- Landlords should take expert legal advice if drafting their own agreements, to avoid clauses being deemed unfair or illegal.

Preparing and signing the tenancy agreement is the main chance for the landlord and tenant to discuss the formal terms of the relationship. Both should have the opportunity to read and understand the terms and each should have a signed copy of the agreement.

If the tenant is moving in immediately, the agreement need not be witnessed, but if they are moving in at a later date, the agreement should be independently witnessed.

Assured shorthold tenancies explained

An assured shorthold tenancy (AST) is considered to be the default letting agreement. If no written contract exists, and there should be any dispute, the tenancy reverts to an AST for legal purposes. The AST covers the legal rights and obligations of the landlord and tenant and can last for any term. Most run for six months, few last more than 12 months.

Many buy to let and HMO mortgage lenders stipulate a maximum 12 month term in their loan terms, so if you want to grant a longer tenancy, check with the lender to make sure the mortgage terms are not breached.

A tenancy agreement restricts the landlord's right to take possession of a property, but gives the benefit of not needing to go to court to obtain possession once the correct notice is served at the end of the AST.

A fixed tenancy is an agreement that gives a tenant a specific date to leave, whereas a periodic or 'rolling' Tenancy does not have a fixed end date.

If a landlord does want tenants to leave, the notice period is generally two months. Within an AST with a specified term, tenants also usually have to give two months' notice; if it has been extended beyond the original term and has become periodic/rolling, tenants typically give one month's notice to move out.

Landlords must ask the tenant to quit by serving a Section 21 notice, and if the tenant then refuses to leave they can seek eviction through the courts. If the tenant has breached terms of the tenancy, the landlord may be able to issue a Section 8 notice. Legal advice should be sought before issuing either, as the correct paperwork must be issued, in the right order, at the right time.

Licence to occupy

Under a licence, tenants' rights to remain are reduced. Licences to occupy are generally for hotels, lodgers, and those in service accommodation. They give someone the right to occupy a room with a property but not to exclusively use communal areas. The landlord may freely come and go from the property (excepting the tenant's room), subject to allowing the tenant the right to 'peaceful enjoyment'.

Unfair terms in tenancy agreements

The Unfair Terms in Consumer Contracts Regulations 1999 covers tenancy agreements and protects the rights of tenants.

A term is unfair if the wording gives the landlord and unfair advantage over the tenant in one of several ways, for example:

- Taking away rights the tenant should generally expect when renting a property
- Any penalty or charge listed in a tenancy agreement must be reasonable in both the amount charged and how it is incurred
- A landlord cannot say a tenant can only do something with written consent, without also saying "consent will not be unreasonably withheld"
- Agreements that are too complicated may be judged invalid by a court

Specific conditions can still be included in the agreement, but they must be written in reasonable terms.

For example, many landlords ban pets as they can cause damage or cause additional wear and tear. Instead of laying down "no pets allowed", which could be considered an unfair condition, saying "pets allowed with the express written permission of the landlord, which will not be withheld unreasonably" is better.

Then, if a tenant wanted to keep a dog, this could be turned down because the noise may inconvenience other tenants, but an aquarium for tropical fish; this is unlikely to upset other tenants and is a more reasonable request.

Always consult a specialist lettings legal professional before adding or removing any terms in a tenancy agreement.

Taking and protecting deposits

Taking a deposit at the start of the tenancy is good practice, so that you have money 'in reserve' in case the tenant causes damage or defaults on their rent and refuses to pay. Almost all landlords ask for one.

This money is then placed 'on protection' with a government authorised scheme and returned to the tenant after they move out, either in full or less any deductions for damage that is beyond fair wear and tear.

The amount of the deposit varies between landlords and often depends on the monthly rent. Many landlords charge one month's rent, some charge a month's rent plus a set amount, others charge six weeks' rent. In effect, it is up to the landlord to decide how much of a deposit to ask for. In the case of HMOs, where people are generally living month to month, a higher level of deposit may put some off and be more money than they can access on move in, so think carefully and do some research before asking for more than a month's deposit.

Also, note that deposits of more than two months' rent give tenants extra rights.

Tenant deposit protection

All deposits taken under an assured shorthold tenancy agreement after April 6, 2007, or under agreements renewed since that date, must be protected.

Deposits for other types of tenancies are not subject to the same rules.

Tenancy deposit protection (TDP) schemes are aimed at safeguarding money a landlord holds for a tenant.

A key point is the deposit belongs to the tenants at all times, not the landlords, even though the money may be in their bank accounts. Placing the deposit on protection reassures tenants that they will get their money back, providing they do not break any terms of the letting agreement.

If the deposit is not placed on protection within 30 days of the start of the tenancy, the tenant can claim compensation in court. The judge can make an award of between one and three times the deposit value.

As a further sanction, landlords who fail to properly protect a deposit cannot take action in court to repossess a property.

To comply with tenancy deposit protection rules, the landlord must give the tenant a written notice of 'prescribed information', explaining:

- Details of the deposit protection scheme
- Information about the scheme's arbitration service in the event of a dispute about returning the deposit
- How the deposit is released at the end of a tenancy
- How the deposit is protected

- Confirmation of the amount paid and the rental property address
- The landlord's contact details
- What the deposit covers
- An explanation of how some or all of the deposit may be kept by the landlord
- How tenants can dispute deductions from the deposit

The available deposit protection schemes

The four government approved deposit protection schemes for England and Wales are:

- Deposit Protection Service - depositprotection.com
- MyDeposits - mydeposits.co.uk
- Tenancy Deposit Scheme - tds.gb.com
- Capita Tenancy Deposit Protection - capita-tdp.co.uk - (not accepting new deposits and closing on 13th September 2014)

There are insurance based options, where you retain the deposit, but pay an amount to insure its security, and custodial schemes, where you pay the deposit over into the scheme's own bank account. Which you choose is down to personal preference.

Review: Chapter 10 of 'HMO PROPERTY SUCCESS':

Part two: Checking your tenant and checking them in

Referencing

The degree to which you reference your prospective tenant may be dictated by your mortgage lender, but may be entirely your decision.

If I was renting out a whole property on a single AST for at least six months, then I'd certainly carry out credit checks and take up references, but when someone's only renting a room in a house, it seems a bit of a waste of time. I take a month's deposit, ask them to complete a personal information form and trust my instincts.

You can take a copy of their passport or driving license (but check how data protection regulations may affect you) and speak to their employer to confirm their status, but further referencing is simply not a good use of your time and doesn't stop people disappearing without paying their rent. If you're in the HMO business, you have to accept that at some point you will be ripped off by a tenant, but it doesn't happen very often.

Before check in

Once you've received the holding fee from your prospective tenant, you can start preparing the AST. Calculate the deposit still owed and the remaining rent for the current month and make sure that the tenant is clear on the amount they have to either bring with them in cash on the day the move in, or transfer in advance.

The two other things it's important to make clear in advance are:

1. individuals' belongings are not covered by your insurance, so the tenant must make their own arrangements if they want cover
2. the TV licence only covers the communal area, so if the tenant wants to have a TV in their room, they're responsible for arranging their own licence.

Check in

If, for any reason, the tenant doesn't settle the full amount due, don't check them in and tell them they'll have to rearrange for another day, once they do have all the money. As a general rule, when room renters fall behind with their payment, they rarely get back on track, so you absolutely don't want to start like that.

Assuming the money side is fine, go through the agreement, highlighting any particularly relevant conditions and restrictions, such as no smoking, notice periods and room access. Sign two copies of the agreement and have the tenant do the same. Confirm the monthly rent and give them a standing order form with your bank details on, for future payments. Always ask your tenants to pay by standing order – it's quick, easy and means there is a clear record on your bank statement. You can waste a lot of time trying to identify cash payments, sometimes not quite for the full amount, that appear in your bank without any reference.

Lastly, there's the inventory. Using an independent inventory clerk when it's only a room check in isn't really worth the cost, although you may want to use a clerk the first time so that you have a professional template. I now use an app on my tablet computer that allows me to take lots of photos and add written descriptions, then I email the whole document to the tenant.

Whatever you decide, you need to make sure you've detailed the condition of the ceiling, walls, floor/carpet, fixtures and fittings and all the contents. Any damage must be clearly specified and I'd suggest you take a photograph of anything significant so there's no argument at a later date. Also note on the inventory how many keys the tenant has been given and make sure you both sign the document. You must also give the tenant information on the scheme you're using to protect their deposit.

After you've checked them in and made sure they know where everything is and how white goods, etc. work, make sure you file all the paperwork, update your records and lodge their deposit funds with your chosen deposit protection scheme.

The importance of inventories

Taking a comprehensive property inventory is a key aspect of managing an HMO.

The inventory is a snapshot of the condition and contents of the property on the day the tenant moves in.

Another inventory is taken on move out day, and the two are compared. Taking into account fair wear and tear, any damage is billed to the tenant.

Taking the inventory

A landlord or letting agent can take the inventory, or sometimes a landlord hires a professional inventory taker. Landlords should only use inventory clerks who are accredited by the Association of Independent Inventory Clerks.

The inventory should accurately reflect the state of the home and should be conducted with the tenant and signed by both the tenant and the landlord. Both parties should retain a copy of the inventory, along with any photographs or video referred to in the document.

Tenancy deposit protection arbitrators are more likely to agree the retention of a deposit by the landlord if the evidence is gathered by an independent third party, such as a letting agent or inventory clerk.

Tips for a perfect inventory

- Be systematic – start at the front door and work through the property room by room, from the ceiling down to the floor. Don't forget garages, sheds and basements.

- List every item, down to the last teaspoon

- Photograph all items – including any scuffs, marks or imperfections, and place a ruler alongside to show scale. This will make it easier to see if damage is worse when the tenant leaves.

- Go through the inventory with the tenant and let them sign and date the final list

- Provide the tenant with a copy

- If any repair work is to be carried out, agree this and record on the inventory what action was taken

Property guides

Property guides are a great way for landlords to minimise the number of general day to day queries from tenants about the HMO.

The guide – ideally a box file or ring binder – should include things such as: copies of manuals for electrical appliances and details of how the boiler works; who to call if any appliance is not working; and where to switch off electricity, water and gas in an emergency.

It is also useful to include other information that a 'fit and proper' HMO manager should pass on to tenants, such as how to deal with rubbish, parking and acceptable behaviour in and around the property.

CHECKLIST

Marketing & letting your rooms

Looking for tenants

☐ Checked out other landlords' adverts online

☐ Created a checklist for taking prospective tenants' information for viewings

☐ Looked into credit referencing agencies

☐ Established a reasonable holding fee and deposit amount

Legal paperwork

☐ Found a local lettings legal specialist / solicitor

☐ Drawn up a suitable, legal tenancy agreement

☐ Chosen a Tenancy Deposit Scheme

☐ Chosen an inventory clerk or drawn up a suitable inventory template for your rooms

Moving a tenant in

☐ Established a process for check in (checklist on next page)

MOVING A TENANT IN CHECKLIST
(Available to download at nickfox.co.uk)

If you use the services of an agent or property manager, they will have a process in place, and most inventory clerks will offer a full check in service. However, if you are handling check ins yourself, you need to make sure everything is done in the correct order and that all necessary paperwork is completed.

This is the process my property manager uses for a new tenant:

Prior to move in

☐ Taken holding fee for the room (receipted if paid in cash)

☐ Agreed move in date and time with the tenant

☐ Forwarded a copy of the tenancy agreement to the tenant, along with a personal information form for them to complete, and advised them they will need to arrange their own TV licence and contents insurance

☐ Made sure the room has been professionally cleaned

Move in day

☐ Gone through the tenancy agreement and confirmed current charges and house rules

☐ Retained one copy of agreement and given one to the tenant, both signed by both parties

☐ Received the tenant's completed personal information form

☐ Given the tenant a Standing Order mandate for them to complete and pass on to their bank

☐ Taken and receipted the deposit balance

☐ Taken and receipted the (balance of) first month's rent

☐ Gone through the inventory with the tenant and secured two signed copies, one to be retained by the tenant

☐ Noted keys on the inventory report and handed them over to the tenant

Following move in

☐ Lodged deposit with chosen deposit protection scheme

☐ Filed paperwork

☐ Diarised agreement end date

PART EIGHT: MANAGING YOUR HMO

After your tenants have moved in, you are obliged to not only keep accurate financial and administrative records, but also to fulfil your responsibilities to the tenants in terms of property maintenance, responding to issues raised and ensuring all AST / license agreement matters are dealt with in the correct legal manner, especially when it comes to ending a tenancy. This part covers the key factors in successfully managing your HMO on an on going basis, so that you continue to realise the best returns on your investment.

The work doesn't stop when tenants move into a letting property; quite the reverse, it's only just begun. Unless landlords employ a letting agent on a fully managed service, they face queries, problems, paperwork and all manner of other tasks on a regular basis.

Many struggle to cope, especially if they have a full time job and family to look after.

The key to success is to try to prepare for every possible situation. Like it or not, sooner or later there will be a tenant who does not pay the rent, a complaint from a neighbour about noise, a broken washing machine or a room that needs redecorating.

By putting an effective procedure in place for dealing with these issues and events, HMO landlords can reduce the stress they face.

Chapter 11 of 'HMO PROPERTY SUCCESS': Managing your HMO

Once your property is tenanted, it needs managing – and HMOs more than any other kind of buy to let – so the key to doing it successfully is organisation. As your business grows, you'll be able to bring on staff to deal with the day to day management, but chances are you'll be doing it yourself in the beginning.

Your maintenance team

Having a good team of contractors is key to managing maintenance issues and making sure they don't escalate into major problems. When little things aren't fixed and tenants feel they're being ignored, it creates a lot of bad feeling, so you need to know your team will act quickly.

One of the most useful people to be able to call on is a really good handyman, who can take care of all sorts of jobs around the property and also be the first port of call if there's a problem with the boiler or electrics, rather than you incurring a callout charge from your plumber or electrician. Tenants tend to be quick to complain without having a proper look at the problem and it's often nowhere near as big an issue as they reported, or something they've inadvertently done, like turning off an electric oven at the mains socket. Even if there is a serious problem and your plumber or electrician can't get to the property until the next day, sending your handyman round to give the tenants peace of mind that something's being done usually goes a long way to keeping them happy.

And you can keep your team happy by paying them quickly. One of the biggest complaints you hear from self employed contractors is about clients taking too long to settle invoices. If they know that you'll always pay when you say you will and you don't mess them around, they'll be loyal to you. Thank them for jobs well done and make sure you remember them at Christmas time.

Regular checks

There are a number of checks that have to be carried out at regular intervals, so you need to set up some kind of diary alert to make sure you don't miss them:

- **Routine inspections.** You'll be seeing some of the property on a reasonably regular basis, as you check tenants in and out and deal with any other issues, but you should make formal inspections of the whole property at least twice a year. You'll need to give the tenants at least 24 hours' written notice that you're going to be entering their rooms and try to do it at a time when they're not there, so you're not disturbing them. Note anything that needs updating, repairing, replacing or replenishing so you can schedule the work, e.g. repainting a hallway or buying some more plates. Write to the tenants to let them know your findings, tell them about any work that's going to be taking place and remind them of their obligations if any clauses in the agreement appear to have been violated, e.g. smoking in the property.
- **Fire alarm testing.** You need to test your fire alarm system regularly, note down the date and results of the test and keep the record separately from the property.
- **Gas safety check.** This must be carried out annually by a Gas Safe registered engineer and the new certificate displayed in the property.
- **Portable Appliance Test (PAT).** All portable electrical appliances (kettle, fridge, TV, etc.) must be tested annually by a qualified engineer.

Change overs

You need to have a slick system in place for when one tenant moves out and another moves in, as it can sometimes happen on the same day. The outgoing tenant needs to be checked out against the move in inventory, then the room needs to be cleaned and made ready for the incoming tenant, who must be checked in with a new AST and inventory. Again, it's down to systemisation, preparation and having a team you can rely on to get things done at the right time.

1. When notice is given, diarise move out day
2. Confirm with tenant that viewings will be taking place and that they'll vacate the room by 12 noon on their last day
3. Check room to estimate any repairs/updating that will be needed
4. Confirm handyman (if necessary) for 12 noon on changeover day and cleaner for 2/3pm
5. Re advertise the room
6. Confirm with new tenant that they can move in after 5pm
7. Prepare new AST and inventory
8. Take original inventory to morning checkout, go through it with tenant, agree any deductions from the deposit, take back keys and note a forwarding address
9. Handyman / cleaner prepare room
10. Check in new tenant with balance of move in monies, AST, inventory and keys
11. Return deposit to former tenant and lodge deposit for new tenant

Obviously, if there are any serious repairs to be carried out, you might need to postpone the move in for a day, or agree with the new tenant what work will be carried out and when.

Even with the best preparation in the world, this won't always run like clockwork – some people are late, others are early – but I've never had any major issues. People are, for the most part, reasonable and small delays can usually be smoothed over.

Refreshing and updating the property

It's generally the case that when you put someone in a nice environment, they'll treat it nicely. Conversely, if you put a tenant into a shabby property that looks as though you don't really care about it – maybe because you're not the one who has to live in it – they're not going to bother looking after it either.

You'll pick up things that need doing when you carry out your quarterly or six monthly property inspections, but ask your property manager, cleaner and handyman to let you know if they think something could do with refreshing or replacing while they're going about their business in the meantime. Sometimes paintwork needs a touch up, the bathroom could do with a new shower curtain or a carpet would benefit from some professional cleaning. If you can make on going improvements before the tenants even notice or think about mentioning them, they'll really appreciate it and, as well as treating the property well, they'll be less likely to complain about little things.

It's not just décor – refresh your appliances as well. If you buy the more budget range kettles, toasters and microwaves, they may not be as hard wearing as more expensive models, but you can afford to throw them out and buy new ones every couple of years. Regardless of how much you've spent on a kitchen appliance and how hard wearing it is, when six people are regularly using it, it suffers wear and tear and starts to look shabby.

And it's the same with larger items of furniture. Budget on the basis that you'll probably replace sofas and armchairs every five or six years because, while they might still be usable, they'll be looking tired. If you want to keep charging top level rents as more recently refurbished properties (including some of your own) come on to the lettings market, you have to keep your HMO looking smart.

Handling tenant issues

Following on from what I said above, if you treat tenants with respect, they'll usually reciprocate. Of course, there will always be the occasional problem tenant, but there's a lot you can do to mitigate the chances of issues flaring up or non payment of rent.

It really comes down to communication and ensuring the tenants feel they're being listened to – don't ever ignore a complaint. If it's a maintenance issue they're complaining about, then your contractors should be able to deal with that fairly quickly. If they can't, find out when they will be able to get to the property and let the tenants know.

When a tenant is either consistently late paying their rent each month or has stopped paying altogether, it's important you don't let yourself get caught up in any sob stories. This is business, you're not running a charity, and the tenant signed an agreement to the effect that they would pay their rent on time every month. Give them a few days to pay everything they owe, then issue them with a Section 8 Notice to Quit and start advertising their room.

Nine times out of ten, this results in the tenant leaving without any further discussion (and also without paying the rent they owe – but their deposit should go some way to reimbursing you for the lost rent), but very occasionally they'll dig their heels in, seek advice from an organisation such as Shelter and refuse to leave. In that case, you can try to reason with them and assure them that if they leave you won't pursue them for what they owe; if that doesn't work, you'll have to begin eviction proceedings.

I'd strongly advise you consider using the services of an eviction specialist (or solicitor), rather than trying to handle it yourself. There is a particular order to the paperwork and a specific way things need to be done and if you get one of the elements wrong, the tenant could claim illegal eviction and you could be forced to begin the process all over again. For the amount they cost, eviction specialists are worth every penny. I should stress, though, it's extremely rare for a tenant in an HMO to see this all the way through to court. They're far more likely to back down and leave when they realise you're serious about the eviction proceedings.

What's sometimes more difficult to deal with is a serious problem between two or more of the house sharers. One of the most common complaints you'll get is about noise – one tenant being inconsiderate and repeatedly shouting, crashing about or playing loud music very late at night, disturbing other tenants. If it's several against one, then you can go ahead and give the culprit a warning about breaking the terms of their agreement, but if it's just one person's word against another, you can't be biased.

Issues like that can self regulate, i.e. the tenant tones down their behaviour or chooses to leave as they're not getting on with the rest of the house, or the problem may need to be escalated. Don't hesitate to call the police if you're at all concerned about things getting out of control, and make sure your tenants know they can do the same. That might sound extreme, but you're a professional landlord, not there to arbitrate in personal disputes or take on someone who's causing a disturbance and possibly breaking the law. Having the police deal with these issues will ensure you and your other tenants aren't endangering your own safety and make it clear to everyone that such behaviour won't be tolerated.

Rents and credit control

Landlords who have followed the tenant finding and referencing procedures set out in the last part will mitigate their cash flow and rent problems. However, even if you think you have the perfect tenants, problems do arise every now and then.

Tenants have a responsibility to ensure that rent is paid in full and on time, as set out in the tenancy agreement. Landlords should not have to chase late payments, but if the rent is not paid promptly every month, it can quickly become a cash flow issue, so must be tackled right away.

Setting out a clear credit control policy at the start of an HMO business is better than waiting for the problem to arise.

The chances of tenants slipping into arrears can be reduced by setting out the rent policy clearly at the start of the tenancy and enforcing the rules at every step along the way.

Make it clear to tenants that they are obliged to pay in full and on time and that this forms part of the tenancy agreement. Explain what will happen if they miss a payment or persistently pay late and ensure they sign the agreement to say they have read and received the information.

In the end, the only good tenant is one who pays the rent in full and on time.

Dos and don'ts of rent collection

As the landlord, how you run your business is largely up to you, provided you adhere to your legal and financial obligations.

If the rent stops for any reason, you will have to find money from elsewhere to pay the mortgage and bills, so do you have enough spare cash to finance the property if tenants get into arrears?

Even the best businesses flounder when they are short of liquid cash, so consider these key tips when it comes to rents:

- Match rent collection with the tenant's pay day, leaving a couple of days' grace for the funds clearing their bank

- If renting to students, consider asking them to pay rent for a block of months at a time on student loan pay days, which are generally in September, January and April. The precise date varies each year according to term start dates.

- Ask tenants to set up a standing order, so they do not have to remember to transfer the money each month

- If the rent is not paid on the due date, speak to the tenant calmly and establish why the payment has not been made. The fault may lie with someone else.

- Consider whether a late payment fee is reasonable. If the rent is only a day or two late, collecting a fee is time consuming and can harm the landlord/tenant relationship.

- However, if tenants take too long to pay, you could soon start to struggle to find the money for the bills and mortgage. Just make sure charge is fair and transparent in the tenancy agreement.

- Do not accept part payments. This can indicate that you accept the lower amount and negates any court notices already served.

Rent books
If rent is paid weekly, then you must issue the tenant with a rent book to comply with the law. Most stationery shops sell rent books. Record each payment in the book and make sure the tenant signs and dates a receipt showing the rent was paid/received.

Collecting cash
Collecting cash from tenants is not generally a good idea, as it is easy for misunderstandings to occur over how much was paid and when.

Keep the property business money in a separate bank account from any personal cash and ask the tenants to make any payments into this account.

This also makes keeping good financial records easier for accounting and tax.

Managing arrears and late payments

Late payments are rents received in full, but after the due date.

Arrears are short or missed payments. Most lenders consider arrears serious when they are late by three months or more because experience shows that a borrower has trouble catching up with more than three months of debt.

Late payment or arrears can happen for a wide range of reasons, including loss of a job and sickness, but do be aware that a tenant may simply be trying to avoid paying altogether.

If tenants miss a payment, wait a couple of days to see if they get in touch or the money arrives and then speak to them about the reasons. Try to have the conversation on email, so you both have a written record of what was said, should the matter go to a court at a later date.

If the tenant is unwilling to or cannot pay the rent, then landlords must consider ending the tenancy to protect their cash flow.

Collecting rent from tenants on Housing Benefit

Landlords who let to tenants claiming housing allowance should make themselves familiar with Universal Credit.

Some councils will delay payments if the landlord or tenant does not fill out applications, or if they are incorrectly completed.

If a tenant meets with financial hardship they may need to consider making a claim for Universal Credit. Landlords should be sensitive about this and offer support, as having the rent paid is in their best interest. There is no legal requirement for landlords to help tenants with benefit claims, but do check the application has been made and help chase the progress.

Contacting guarantors

If a guarantor has signed the tenancy agreement, then they have consented to pay the rent for the tenant if the tenant is unable or unwilling to do so.

This also applies to bills for cleaning, damage to the property and any other tenant obligations.

Guarantors are contractually bound to accept the liability and can be taken to court if they refuse to do so.

If the tenant does not pay the rent, then contact the guarantor and explain the situation to them and the likely consequences of the rent remaining unpaid. This generally resolves the issue.

Be careful to follow the law, which means not making unfair charges or harassing the tenant or guarantor.

One tip here is to always look for a guarantor who is a homeowner. They are less likely to move and have more to lose if the case goes to court and a judgment is listed against them.

Visiting the property

Landlords or their letting agent should visit the let property every 3-6 months to check for maintenance issues and to make sure the tenant is keeping to the tenancy agreement.

Maintenance visits and access for gas, fire and electrical safety checks should be arranged as necessary.

Unless a tenant agrees otherwise, the landlord must give 24 hours' notice of a visit and explain the purpose of the visit.

Landlords should never enter the tenant's home without permission and, preferably, with the tenant or someone representing them being present. Landlords are legally obliged to maintain their HMO in a reasonable state of repair and local authorities can take enforcement action if they identify any risks under the Housing Health and Safety Rating System within the Housing Act 2004.

Tenants should understand these maintenance checks are necessary to keep them safe and their home compliant with the terms of any HMO licence.

Any terms in the tenancy agreement about access and inspections must be reasonable.

Tenants have the right to quiet enjoyment of their home and may refuse access, even if notice is given.

Landlords should try to find out why access was denied before taking legal action to enter or possess the property.

Entering tenant areas

The conditions above apply to areas where the tenant or tenants in a joint tenancy have exclusive access, such as bedrooms, personal storage areas and en suites.

Entering common areas

Landlords can access communal areas that remain under their control at reasonable hours, but notice should still be given if the visit or any work is likely to cause inconvenience to tenants.

Emergency access

In an emergency, landlords and contractors can enter a property without permission from the tenant.

Unlawful harassment

Harassment is a criminal offence under the Protection from Harassment Act 1997.

Harassment is defined as:

- Interfering with the peace and comfort of a tenant
- Persistent withdrawal of essential services with the intention of making the tenant leave their home or stopping them pursuing their legal rights

For example, harassment could include:

- Threats of violence or unlawful eviction
- Disconnecting gas, electricity or water supplies without good reason
- Breaking a key in a lock to stop a tenant entering their home
- Deliberately disruptive repair works
- Frequent visits at unreasonable hours
- Entering the property without the tenant's permission

Landlords who harass tenants can face fines of up to £5,000 – and even imprisonment.

Any letter from a tenant, lawyer or local authority alleging harassment should be taken seriously.

Landlords should take detailed notes of all meetings and conversations with tenants and follow advice given by council housing officers. They should also seek legal advice.

Tenants can also make a claim to the County Court for an injunction to reinstate them in the property and can claim damages.

Dealing with repairs and complaints

It's a good idea to have a policy for dealing with repairs and complaints from the start of the tenancy.

Again, if a landlord has a letting agent managing the property, they should be the point of first contact. Generally, most letting agents ask landlords to agree an authorised figure (usually up to £100) that can be spent on resolving minor issues.

Landlords who manage their properties themselves should give tenants clear contact instructions, including for out of hours emergencies. Both phone and email details should be provided.

Prioritising repairs is important for landlords and tenants. Problems with heating, hot water and the electrics should be handled as soon as possible, but replacing a lampshade or hanging a picture can wait a little longer.

Telephone or email hotline

Many landlords have a pay as you go mobile phone for calls from tenants, or free email (such as Googlemail or Hotmail) set up for each property in a portfolio to sort messages.

Set up a line of communication with tenants, including an emergency telephone contact, and explain when to use each and how they are monitored.

For real emergencies, like gas or water leaks, cut out the 'middle man' and give the tenant a direct contact number for the utility service.

How to respond to calls from tenants

Whenever a tenant gets in touch, acknowledge their message and explain what you are going to do in response. Do not create unnecessary upset by suggesting that they need to stop hassling you.

The problem being reported may seem trivial to you, but the tenant is paying to live in your property and wants to feel safe and comfortable.

Some landlords specify that tenants can only ring between certain times of the day.

A reasonable cut off time for calls is 7pm Monday to Friday, except in an emergency. This gives the tenant time to get home from work and discover a problem. To avoid misunderstandings, define clearly for the tenant what constitutes an emergency and what is considered a repair that can wait.

If a tenant works shifts, arrange a contact time that suits you both.

Sending contractors

Tenants have a right to privacy, so neither a landlord nor workmen can turn up at any time they like and expect to gain access. (**If tenants are on a license agreement, access can be gained to the communal areas at any time, although this must not violate tenants' rights to quiet enjoyment of the property.)

Tenants should have at least 24 hours' notice of any appointment, except in an emergency.

You may find it easier to ask permission to give the tenant's number to the workman and let them sort out a suitable access time between them.

If a tenant is not allowing reasonable access and the problem could lead to more expense, then the landlord has a right to minimise the damage. The tenancy agreement should set out how such situations are managed.

Common problems / issues

Some problems and complaints are common, particularly in the communal areas of an HMO. Landlords should check these regularly and have an action plan for dealing with any complaints.

Lighting

It is not unreasonable to expect tenants to replace normal light bulbs, but not in homes with high ceilings, as they may fall off a chair. Special fittings, such as halogen lamps and LED bulbs, can be tricky to handle.

Landlords should keep a supply of these bulbs in the properties and have a handyman change them as required.

Beeping smoke alarms

A smoke alarm that constantly beeps is usually a sign of a faulty or flat battery. Landlords must install and maintain smoke detectors and heat sensors, including testing and replacing batteries as required.

Alarm systems that run off the mains may be a more convenient option and may be required under the terms of an HMO licence. Long life batteries for smoke alarms are also available. The local fire service can advise on smoke alarms and fire safety and will sometimes fit basic alarms for free.

Rubbish disposal

Provide tenants with information on rubbish disposal and collection. These days most homes have a wheelie bin for general rubbish, and a selection of boxes for recycling and waste.

Tenants who do not dispose of rubbish according to council guidelines or put their bins out too far ahead of collection days can be fined.

With an average of 5 or 6 adults in one property, it is common for HMOs to produce a high level of rubbish. Speak to your local council, explain the level of occupancy in the property and make sure they are providing the largest rubbish and recycling bins permissible – generally a 240L size.

Condensation

Condensation often results from drying clothes inside without adequate ventilation.

Landlords can either provide a dryer or request that tenants not to dry their clothes inside without opening windows. Landlords should also point out that rooms should be aired regularly by opening windows, to stop damp and mould building up.

Use mould resistant paint in bathrooms and kitchens and factor into your maintenance plan for a handyman to periodically apply anti mould spray in areas where condensation has a tendency to build up.

Heating & plumbing

If left to their own devices, tenants may be tempted to fiddle with boiler settings. It is advisable to conceal both the boiler controls and the thermostat behind locked panels, so that only you and any authorized contractors can gain access.

Blocked sinks or drains are common, particularly in houses where several people shower and wash up each day.

Landlords should explain to tenants not to dispose of food waste down the sink and ask that tenants clear pipes of hair and dirt regularly Sometimes problems still arise and these should be dealt with quickly by a plumber.

In hard water areas, it is also advisable to instruct the cleaner or handyman to de-scale showerheads every 6 to 8 weeks, to avoid problems arising, particularly in the case of electric shower units.

Redecorating and hanging pictures

A common request from tenants is to hang pictures or redecorate rooms. In most cases, putting up a picture or changing curtains is a reasonable request and should not be refused, but landlords may stipulate that such additions or changes are limited.

If a room is in need of redecorating as a matter of course, this is the landlord's responsibility. But if the tenant just 'fancies a change', it is up to the landlord whether this can be done. Landlords can stipulate acceptable colours and specify whether the work must be carried out by a professional painter / decorator.

As a general rule, all walls and paintwork should be kept neutral.

Broadband, cable and satellite TV
A landmark ruling in the European Court of Justice set a precedent for human rights for tenants in rental properties.

A family wanted satellite TV, but the landlord refused permission for a dish on the outside of the property. The family claimed that this infringed their human rights by restricting their right to access information without interference.

The court agreed and ruled against the landlord, ordering him to pay compensation of £12,000.

The ruling places a burden on landlords to let tenants have broadband, cable and satellite TV in the communal living area.

 **It should be noted that if tenants want televisions in their rooms, they are responsible for their own TV licence – the one paid for by the landlord only covers the communal TV.

Handling problem tenants

However many checks and references a landlord carries out (see 'selecting tenants' in PART SEVEN), sooner or later, everyone has a tenant who causes problems.

Some tenants are simply difficult by nature, while others fall into difficulties due to job loss, illness or other personal problems.

All you can do as a landlord is to have a procedure to put into operation when something starts to go wrong, and the key is addressing problems early and in a calm manner.

Rent arrears
Tenants paying their rent late or missing payments completely is a relatively common problem for landlords. People renting rooms are often living month to month and so can easily find themselves short if they have not been able to work for some reason, or they have had an unexpected expense, such as a dentist's bill or car repairs.

Housing groups, including Shelter, talk about 'rogue landlords' and their shabby treatment of tenants, but fail to mention the tenants who seem to treat their rent as an unauthorised overdraft to dip into for treats and holidays.

Tenants who do not pay rent are not good tenants.

The point a landlord needs to establish is whether the rent problem is a one off or an issue that is likely to persist.

If the rent is a couple of days late, the first step is to talk to the tenant to find out what the problem is. Sometimes the issue is just one of those things – they may have been paid late or the bank may have made a mistake.

If they have a cash flow problem, agree a payment schedule with them and put it in writing, and if they then miss one of those payments, you may need to begin eviction proceedings. Unfortunately, when HMO tenants fall behind with their rent, the majority are unable to ever make it up, so the most sensible financial move for you is to get them out of the property as soon as legally possible, so that you can get a full paying tenant in.

'Ghost' tenants moving in without permission

Ghost tenants – those who are not named on the tenancy agreement – are a real headache for landlords.

Recent research by insurance company Direct Line estimates that more than 3 million of these ghost tenants may live in private rented homes without permission.

The issue is important for licensed HMO landlords, as their licences will specify the number of people who can live in a property. If this number is exceeded, the HMO manager is in breach of licence conditions and could face prosecution. Not only that, but too many people living in an HMO can lead to excessive wear and tear on the property and problems with extra rubbish and parking.

Landlords should keep a check on who lives at a shared house and, if a tenant moves a friend or partner in, quick action should be taken to make sure HMO licensing terms are not broken and the right amount of rent is collected.

Anti social behaviour

Anti social behaviour does not have a clear definition, but essentially is any activity that causes annoyance to others. It is fairly common with HMOs that at some point tenants will complain about each other or neighbours will report issues.

Any reports of anti social behaviour should be taken seriously and acted on.

The most common complaint is about noise, with reports of drunkenness, litter and drug usage also to be expected from time to time.

If there are any reports of drug usage, that is a police matter and you should make it clear that the presence of drugs in the house will not be tolerated. Do not hesitate to call the police to investigate if you become aware of it yourself and assure the tenants that you will support them in doing the same.

If a particular tenant is repeatedly causing problems, it may be sensible to give them a warning and then, if their anti social behaviour persists, ask them to leave and begin eviction proceedings if necessary. Bad tenants in a shared house can cause other good tenants to leave.

It's a good idea to discuss issues with the local authority, police and your local landlords association. If the tenants are students, approaching the university student union may help.

Ending a Tenancy

Sooner or later, either tenants will want to move out themselves or the landlord will want them to leave, even if the tenants are happy in the property and no problems or disputes have arisen.

Tenants may want to move in with a partner, buy their own property, rent a home of their own or simply be moving out of the area.

As with all other aspects of letting an HMO, landlords must have a procedure in place for when a tenant moves out, to make the process as simple as possible for both parties and ensure there are no problems when the time comes to take the property back.

Landlords must be prepared for final inspections, know what to do with the deposit, and consider marketing for a new tenant.

The tenancy agreement should outline what tenants and landlords have to do ahead of moving out and also clearly state that the property must be returned in the same condition as when rented out, allowing for reasonable wear and tear.

Landlords and tenants can terminate assured shorthold tenancies in a number of ways. The end date of the agreement should be noted and both parties' intentions should be discussed about three months before the end of the agreement.

If you want the tenant to move out, you can give them two months' notice to quit.

If the tenant wants to move out, there are different rules depending on the agreement in place and whether the contract has ended and become a periodical tenancy, or is still within the original time (usually 6 months). They should generally give 2 months' notice, although many HMO landlords accept one month's notice.

Housing law, issuing notice to quit and eviction is a complicated area of the law, and landlords should always take professional advice from a specialist lettings lawyer before taking any legal steps.

Making a small error on a form filed with a court can mean a judge throws out the proceedings and the whole process has to start again.

Evicting a tenant

If a tenant faces eviction, a whole mountain of legal challenges must be dealt with. Taking possession of the property must follow the correct legal procedure. If landlords do not follow the rules they can be liable to pay compensation and legal costs.

Under the Protection from Eviction Act 1977, anyone expecting a tenant, their friends or visitors to simply 'give up' accommodation they have entered lawfully, commits an offence.

There are two main routes for taking back possession of a property under assured shortbhold tenancy agreements: the issuing of Section 8 and Section 21 notices.

Section 8

If the landlord wants to get possession before the fixed term comes to an end, he must serve notice of his intention. The rules are set out under Section 8 of the Housing Act 1988. A Section 8 notice is usually served if the landlord considers that the tenant has breached the terms of their agreement.

The requirements for serving Section 8 are:

- The landlord serves notice and proceedings begin within the time limits of the Act and as stated in the notice

- The notice must be given in the prescribed form (templates are available from legal stationers)

- The notice must specify why the landlord requires possession

There are 17 grounds under which the landlord can recover possession under Section 8 and those the case relies on must be clearly stated, along with supporting evidence.

Section 21

Landlords letting with an assured shorthold tenancy agreement have a legal right to take the property back at the end of a tenancy.

This process must follow Section 21 of the Housing Act 1988. Different rules apply to notices served during the fixed term and periodic tenancies.

For more detailed information on issuing section notices, visit the GOV.UK website.

**Remember that, even though you are only letting a room and may be doing so on a licence agreement, the default legal agreement (should any mater end up in court) is taken to be an AST, so it is those rules Landlords should follow for ending a tenancy.

Unlawful eviction
Problem tenants still have legal rights and landlords must be aware of these if they are seeking to evict them. Under the Protection from Eviction Act 1977, unlawfully depriving a 'residential occupier' of their occupation of a home is a criminal offence. Unless the tenant agrees to leave the landlord must obtain a
court order to get them out of the property. As above, in most cases the Act also applies to those living in a property on a licence.

The law lays out a clear eviction process, which must be followed at all times.

Getting the process wrong can be expensive, as landlords risk being accused of harassment and can end up having to pay compensation and legal fees.

Local council housing departments and homeless charities generally see problems from the point of view of the tenant, so landlords must get specialist, independent legal advice from a solicitor before acting.

If a tenant abandons their room
Tenants abandon their home when they leave without giving notice. A typical scenario is when the tenant has built up significant rent arrears and disappears so that they don't have to pay.

Abandonment can create problems for a landlord.

Legally, if the tenant has not given notice to quit, the tenancy is still running and the tenant can come back and live in the home, even if the rent is unpaid. Therefore, from a landlord's point of view, the home cannot legally be let to another tenant.

Failing to follow these rules could lead to a claim for unlawful eviction.

In reality, when a tenant abandons their room in an HMO, they are highly unlikely to return. If they do, and demand re entry, you are entitled to give them any other available room – it does not have to be the same one. But this is a very unlikely scenario. Simply make sure that if they have left any belongings, these are stored securely and all efforts are made to contact the tenant.

If the tenant does not collect their items within three months, they can be sold and the landlord may deduct the costs of storage from the money made. The balance belongs to the tenant and they have six years to claim this money.

Tenants staying on
Most HMO landlords sign tenants on to a fixed term licence or tenancy agreement.

At the end of the agreement, if the landlord does nothing and the tenant remains in the property, then the agreement will automatically run on from one rent period to the next on the same terms.

This is a statutory periodic tenancy and continues until a new agreement is signed, the tenant moves out, or the landlord is awarded possession of the property by the courts.

Students who wish to stay in the property over the summer can do so, but it is sensible for landlords to enquire about their intentions as early as possible so decisions about repairs and marketing can be taken.

Managing check-out day

Tenants may not always follow the exact conditions of the tenancy agreement as they prepare to move out. They are usually more concerned with packing up belongings and moving into their next home.

Nevertheless, both sides must meet their obligations when move out day arrives.

Make sure you give the tenant clear information, in writing, on what is expected from them before they hand back the keys and ensure they understand their rights and obligations for the end of tenancy so there are no misunderstandings.

Checking the property

Schedule the final inspection for after the tenant has removed all their furniture and belongings. This will help ensure that no belongings or rubbish are left behind and allows landlords to clearly see any damage or defects. Ideally, ask for them to have the room cleared by 12 noon, in order to give you enough time to have it cleaned and repaired if necessary, then move a new tenant in either after 5pm or the next day.

Not all tenants will want to wait for this inspection, but it is wise to encourage them to do so. Explain that it is important you both agree on any problems or damage they have caused and how much of the deposit might be retained, to avoid disputes at a later date.

Go through their room and check off everything on the original inventory, making notes and taking photographs of any discrepancies.

Normal wear and tear...

The phrase 'normal wear and tear' is not explained in law and, if a case does go before the Property Ombudsman or the courts, the outcome will be dependent on the merits of each individual case.

Landlords must accept that wear and tear occurs simply as a result of people living in a property and tenants cannot be expected to pay for this when they move out. Carpets will become worn, paintwork may scuff, etc., and in HMOs, where a number of people are coming and going, it's usually impossible to attribute wear and tear in communal areas to any one tenant.

However, burns in the carpet or holes in the walls go beyond normal wear and tear.

Speak to tenants about any damage and only charge what is reasonable to repair the problems.

Retaining some or all of the deposit

Landlords can make deductions from a deposit to cover:

- Unpaid rent
- Damage beyond normal wear and tear
- Replacing lost keys or locks
- Cleaning

If the landlord is keeping some or all of the deposit, the tenant should have a detailed report that highlights the damage and the cost of repairs. Tenants can ask for additional quotes to ensure that any charges are reasonable for the work involved.

If the deposit is on protection, charges should be included in the summary statement and the balance of the money then released to the tenant. Is it good practice to return monies via the bank, rather than in cash, and to do so within 30 days.

If rent arrears, repairs and cleaning costs amount to more than the deposit, then landlords may decide to take steps to try to recover the extra money. However, this can be difficult and will often involve a court case, making it an expensive process, which may outweigh the amount of money owed or that can be expected in compensation.

If the tenancy agreement has a guarantor, landlords can approach them for any money owing, as they have the same legal obligations as the tenant.

Although unusual in HMOs, if utility accounts are in the name of the tenant, payment of the final bill is up to them and the suppliers cannot require the landlord to pay. When the tenant moves out, the landlord should notify the suppliers, pass on the agreed final meter reading, the changeover dates and give the name of the new tenant.

Marketing for new tenants

Many HMO landlords with sizeable portfolios keep adverts running all the time, but if you only have one or two HMOs, you must start re marketing in good time – as soon as a tenant has given you notice. Make sure your online adverts have plenty of photographs and that your rent is still competitive.

Legally, you are entitled to carry out viewings while the outgoing tenant is still occupying the room, with 24 hours' notice. When you have issued or received notice that they are leaving, it is good practice to acknowledge this in writing, and you should also ask that they keep their room tidy in readiness for viewings.

However, if there has been any bad feeling or the tenant is particularly messy, you may find you have to explain to prospective tenants that the room will be professionally cleaned, repainted if necessary and any damage repaired, to reassure them that they will have a nice home

Ideally, you should look to move a new tenant in either the same day or the day after the outgoing tenant leaves.

Chapter 12 of 'HMO PROPERTY SUCCESS':
Managing your business

An HMO generates a lot of paperwork and relies on constant figure tracking and analysis, so it's imperative you have a good administration system and a good administrator to manage it. If that's not your forte, then employ someone who can keep on top of everything for you.

General administration

Filing paperwork correctly so it can be located when needed is something of a skill and if you don't do it every one or two days as your business grows, you can easily get in a mess (although some of this paperwork can be 'off loaded' to a bookkeeper periodically). These are just some of the things you'll need to file:

- Purchase and mortgage documentation
- Refurbishment invoices and receipts
- Guarantees
- Utility bills
- Gas and electric certificates
- Tenant paperwork
- Rent receipts
- Bank statements
- Receipts for expenses
- On going maintenance invoices
  …and the list goes on.

Given that you're going to have an average of two tenants checking in and out of each room every year, you also need a good 'dead filing' system for archiving paperwork. As the number of properties you own grows, so does the paperwork, and you might quickly find that the area you originally designated as office space is a bit small Landlords tend to start in a small box room, progress to converting the garage into an office, then realise they need other premises, particularly when they start taking on staff and needing more office equipment, such as better printers, a photocopier, shredder, etc.

You may also find it useful to invest in some lettings software. There are a number of products on the market designed to help you keep track of your business by holding all your property and tenant information in one place.

There are products with facilities for handling bookkeeping and credit control; maintenance schedules can be set up; photographs and documentation relating to each property and tenant can be uploaded, and the system can be set to flag up tenancy and certification renewal dates, reminding you to take action.

Most of these products will have free trial periods, so it may be well worth your while to look at a few different ones and see which you feel could best help your business.

KPIs

I said in Chapter 2 that I focus on three main things: profit, ROI and yield, all of which I'm constantly trying to maximize. Having systemised the business and taken on capable staff to essentially run the day to day operation, I'm free to do what I'm best at: ensure my investments give the best possible return.

Increasing profit

There are only two ways you can increase monthly profit: secure more rental income or/and reduce costs. Let's start with the slightly more straightforward one. You should have a complete breakdown of your costs on your main viability analysis spreadsheet, so it's simply a case of working through those and seeing if any reductions can be made, without asking anyone on your maintenance team to take a pay cut

Your biggest monthly outgoing is always going to be your mortgage, but the costs of switching to a new product can be relatively large, so it's not something I do very often. I have a good relationship with my broker and am confident they're keeping an eye out for a deal worthwhile taking. What you need to focus on yourself are utility and telecom service providers and your insurance provider, and it really is worth getting new quotes every few months and regularly switching to get the best deals. A few pounds saved every month, across all the properties in your portfolio, can stack up to a significant amount every year.

Also keep an eye on your maintenance bills for repairing white goods and make sure you don't end up spending more on fixing them than they're worth. Again, having a good supplier that you can trust to be honest with you about this is a big help. And don't be afraid to ask for discounts for buying multiple units. When suppliers know you're a landlord that's likely to be able to give them regular on going business, there are usually deals to be done with them.

When it comes to securing more rental income, there are three things I look at: increasing rents, increasing occupancy levels and renting things other than simply bedrooms:

1. Increasing rents. This isn't something you can – or should – do just because you think you can. While tenants will pay the best market rents for the best rooms, you need to make sure you don't price yourself out of the market. Keep an eye on what the competition is offering and charging because, while your refurbishment and furnishing might have made your property one of the best in the area when you started out, landlords are providing better and better quality accommodation as time goes on. At the same time, you must try to ensure you increase your rents at least in line with inflation, otherwise your profits are decreasing in real terms. It's a tricky line to walk, though, because you can only charge what people are willing to pay. My advice is to make sure you track the top, bottom and average rents in the area and be aware of inflation, so that you're always able to compare your returns accurately with both local averages and other investments.

2. Increasing occupancy levels. It's virtually impossible to consistently achieve 100% occupancy, but you should certainly be averaging at least 95%. As I've already said, voids will make a big impact on your profit, so you must do everything you can to avoid them. Retaining tenants is the cheapest and easiest solution, so make sure you fix problems quickly, take care of the property and have a good relationship with your tenants so they don't have any reason to leave your property for someone else's. People always move on at some point, but try to keep each tenant for at least 6 months. When tenants do leave, try to have someone ready to move in right away, even if it means taking slightly less rent. That might be contradicting the last point ( ), but you have to consider the implications of having an empty room for a week or two, 'losing' you rent, versus lowering the price by £5 or even £10 a week. It's almost always worth the slight reduction, not only in term of immediate rental income gained, but also because if you have rooms standing empty, existing tenants might start to feel there's something wrong with the property and there's better to be had elsewhere.

3. Renting out other things. I know several landlords who make extra money from renting out garages and box rooms that are too small to use as bedrooms. That might be renting to current tenants or to other people if something like a garage or storage unit is separate from the house. You can also generate additional income through having coin operated washing machines and tumble dryers, although this has to be considered against the rent tenants are already paying for facilities. The

point is, think laterally and make sure you're maximizing the potential of every square foot you've invested in.

Return On Investment

Increased income and reducing costs, as outlined above, will result in a better ROI, but you should also periodically look at the amount of capital tied up in each property and assess whether it might be worth releasing some of it. Back in the early 2000s, when the market was hurtling up, it was often possible to remortgage and release all the capital you'd originally put in – and then some. With the market the way it is at the moment, you're not going to be able to do that, but you could still get some money out after a few years.

In order to work out whether that's a viable and good investment move, your analysis spreadsheet needs to be up to date and set up with the correct formulae so you can immediately see:

1. With the increased mortgage cost, am I still achieving the monthly cash flow I need?
2. Will I be able to invest the money released in such a way that it gives a better return?
3. What is the cost (fees and other charges) of facilitating the equity release?

This is where, again, you'll realise the benefit of having a financial advisor who is also a property investor, because they'll be able to quickly work the figures, understand exactly what it is you need to consider and give you informed, relevant advice. Your knee jerk reaction might be to say that you don't want to increase your mortgage costs because you need the monthly cash flow for income, but what if you could make as much or even more overall from reinvesting some of the capital in another property or even a different investment vehicle?

Ultimately, if you can get to the point where you have none of your own money invested in a property that's still giving you some monthly income, while also appreciating in value, you'll be getting an infinite return on investment.

Yield

Yield is the figure that allows you to see whether you're investing in the right kind of property, both in terms of type and location. Gross yield is the rental income as a percentage of the property's value and net yield is the profit as a percentage of value. I almost never look at other people's gross yield, because it doesn't take into account either how much money is invested or any costs, so is pretty meaningless when you're trying to compare two investments.

For example, because rental income is two to three times higher for HMOs than similar properties rented as single units, the gross yield is significantly higher. A detached house with four bedrooms and three reception rooms, worth £200,000 might rent to a family for £1,000 a month, giving a gross yield figure of 6%, while renting six individual bedrooms might achieve £2,400, giving a gross yield of 14.4%. But if the landlord of the single unit owns the property outright and therefore doesn't have monthly mortgage payments, while the landlord of the HMO is highly geared and has all the additional costs (utility bills, council tax, TV license, increased maintenance, handyman, cleaner, gardener and more management costs), the net yields and monthly cash flow could be not that different. What will be very different is the ROI.

So I'd suggest you forget yield as a tool for comparing your properties' performances to other people's, unless you know that their investment model is the same as yours. What I use net yield for is comparing the properties in my portfolio with each other – that's where it becomes really useful and it's something I'm constantly tracking. My costs don't tend to vary from one HMO of the same size to another, but the property values vary, as does the rental income. Looking at the net yield figures, I can see at a glance which properties in which areas were the better buys, from a cash flow perspective.

Of course, the caveat is that you have to take the yield figure in context with the capital growth figure. The yield figures might suggest you'd be better off selling a property and reinvesting the money into one that has a better income:value ratio, but if the reason for the lower yield figure is that the property has grown in value more than others in your portfolio, it's probably worth holding on to.

Capital Growth

Whether a property grows in value or not is pretty much out of your hands. Yes, you can make sure you maintain it well and could extend, convert or renovate to add value, but once your HMO is up and running, it's in the hands of the market. Nevertheless, you must keep track of what's happening to property values, to make sure that you not only know how much your own portfolio is worth, but also can see which of your properties are growing more quickly in value.

As I said in the section above, you can greatly increase your ROI by refinancing and pulling out some of your invested capital, so keep track of exactly how much equity you have in each property, assuming you'll always need to keep 25% in. Set up your spreadsheet so that you can easily see:

- purchase price
- invested capital
- current value
- total equity
- amount you could pull out (total equity, less 25% of current value)

If certain property types in certain areas have grown more in value over the last few years, look at the economic drivers and what's likely to happen in the future, and that will help you see whether it's worth making further investment there.

Most of the professional landlords I know keep a balanced portfolio, with some properties that generate a high level of monthly income and others that aren't so good on cash flow, but are much better in terms of capital growth. And I'd suggest that tracking your KPIs so you can make sure you consistently maximize your returns in a variety of ways and spread the investment risk, is a very sensible investment strategy.

One more little note…

Of these four key metrics, the one you'll hear investors most often mention is yield. What I'm saying is that yield needs to be taken as just one part of an overall picture that includes profit, ROI and capital growth, and it will be more or less relevant to you, depending on your investment objectives. So if someone says they're getting a better yield than you, understand that the conversation is only just beginning

CHECKLIST

Managing your HMO

☐ Set up business bank account for receiving rents

☐ Purchased a rent book for any cash payments

☐ Set up a system for receiving and handing complaints

☐ Secured tradespeople for on going maintenance:

- ° Handyman for general maintenance
- ° Plumber
- ° Emergency plumber (if different)
- ° Electrician
- ° Emergency electrician (if different)

☐ Understood which Section Notices need to be served and when

☐ Established check out process

Business administration

In addition to the above practicalities, your business administration systems should also be set up by now. To effectively manage your HMO business on an on going basis, you should have:

☐ Made sure your property analysis spreadsheets are up to date & you have diarised:

- ° cost reviews
- ° current property valuations
- ° rent reviews

☐ Understood your key KPIs:

- ° profit
- ° ROI
- ° yield
- ° capital growth

☐ Established what sources can quickly give you a snapshot of the current market

☐ Arranged with your financial advisers how often you will review your business

PART NINE:

PROPERTY TAX FOR HMOs

Property tax is a very specific and complex area of taxation, so you should ensure you engage someone who is a property tax specialist to advise you. The amount you have to pay to HMRC will depend on your own particular situation, including how you legally own your property/ies, your personal earnings, how you allocate expenditure and how and when you take money out of your property business.

This part outlines taxation that may be applied, your obligations to keep accurate records and suggests how you might organise your financial administration. It also covers expenses that may be tax deductible and common allowances.

To reiterate: property tax is not something you should tackle on your own and you should take advice before you buy your first HMO, as correcting things retrospectively can be difficult and expensive. Get an experienced advisor in place as early as possible, and ideally choose someone who has a property portfolio themselves.

HM Revenue and Customs will chase down landlords who do not pay the tax they owe on rental properties, so keeping the finances up to date from day one is a primary task.

The taxman has a variety of tactics to track down those who do not pay their dues. HMRC is linked with other agencies and departments to give a broader picture of a person's assets and income.

The taxman can now access all Land Registry records which, when cross referenced with the electoral roll and council tax data, can show who owns and lives in a property.

This helps HMRC determine whether the property is let and whether rental income should have been declared, and also whether capital gains tax was due on the sale of a property.

Letting agents also report all rents received and who they were paid to each year.

Anyone who breaks the rules can be fined – even if it was simply a mistake - and deliberate tax evasion is a criminal offence.

If you have not dealt with property income, expenditure and tax before, it is highly unlikely that you will be able to maintain your finances in the proper manner, so engage an accountant who can facilitate your bookkeeping and complete your tax returns. This may be via your tax advisor, or could be an independent third party.

Overview of property tax

There is no single property tax. Instead there are several taxes that apply to property owners, including those with buy to lets, second homes and HMOs. The main taxes that landlords have to face are income tax and capital gains tax (CGT).

Income tax is due on rental income and CGT is paid on any increase in the property value during the period of ownership.

Who pays property tax?

The general rule of thumb is that tax follows ownership of an asset. Technically, HMRC will look to the beneficial owner of a property for any tax due on rents or disposal.

A beneficial owner is someone who receives a cut of the rental profits or the disposal value of a property, even if their name is not on the title at the Land Registry.

Paying property tax is not optional and HMRC is cracking down on avoidance and evasion. The obligation is on the person earning the income to report the details to the taxman.

Some income shifting strategies to minimise property tax are available, but do not jump into them without professional advice and careful consideration, and make sure you follow the precise procedures.

When is property tax paid?

Income tax is paid in two installments: January 31 and July 31 of each year.

The tax relates to the property business financial year. The first tax year runs from the date of first letting of the first rental property to the following April 5. If the tenancy starts on April 1, then rather than draft two sets of accounts, include the overhanging few days in the next tax year.

For subsequent years, the tax year runs from April 6 until the following April 5, throughout the life of the business.

A property business ends when the final tenancy agreement ends.

The final tax year runs from April 6 until the date the tenancy agreement finishes.

Inspections by the taxman

HMRC can launch an investigation into tax returns - or a lack of tax returns - at any time. The onus is on landlords to fill out and file their tax return each year, not for HMRC to chase them.

An inspection can be a traumatic process. Landlords will have to dig out and show all their records for the period required, and if these are not properly filed and ordered, this in itself can be incredibly time consuming.

Using an accountant or bookkeeper will make any inspection easier to deal with.

If you fail to tell the tax man about your property...

A typical scenario is a landlord starts with a single buy to let property and makes a rental loss because he has to spend money on refurbishments and his mortgage interest rate is high. No profits were made and therefore no tax is due, so the landlord does not bother to submit a tax return.

Over the next couple of years the landlord buys more properties. His paperwork becomes more time consuming and complicated, but because the taxman has not said anything about the first year, the landlord feels no pressure to submit tax returns and lets them slide.

But HMRC can go back a number of years once a tax inquiry is started. Now the years have passed, the initial rental losses that cancelled out taxable profits have dropped away and the lower mortgage rates now enjoyed by the landlord means the level of expenses claimed has also decreased.

It is likely that the landlord will receive a compliance letter from the taxman, suggesting that he may have had property income that has gone undeclared and requiring that rental accounts for all years in question are prepared. This letter is the start of a tax investigation, during which HMRC will work out how much is owed.

Some inquiries have stretched back to the 1990s, and the stress, time and cost of going back over all this paperwork can be a massive burden on landlords. This is why it is vital that accurate records are maintained from the start of a property business and tax obligations are met in the first tax year.

Interest on unpaid tax accrues at a daily rate and, in some cases, fines and surcharges can run to thousands of pounds.

Again, to avoid falling victim to investigation, ensure you take specialist advice from the outset.

Keeping good financial records

Keeping clear and comprehensive financial records from the start of the property business is vital. If you do not have a system for keeping track of income and expenses as you go along, your paperwork will soon spiral out of control. Leave it too long and it can be a mammoth task to get everything back in order.

Landlords face fines and penalties for not keeping good business records and making mistakes on their tax returns. And if the paperwork is not correct and up to date, you may pay too much or too little tax.

Basic financial records should cover:

- Tenancy agreements
- Rent books
- Bank statements
- Receipts, bills and invoices for business expenses
- Business mileage records
- Finance statements for mortgages, credit cards and loans

Each piece of paper in the file should be clearly labeled and dated.

Setting up business bank accounts

Landlords should have a separate business bank account for their rental business. This same account can be used for several rental properties, but the records must clearly show which payments and receipts are attributable to which property.

Some business bank accounts come with certain charges or conditions and landlords must ensure they choose the one that best suits their needs. Speak to several banks about your requirements before opening an account, to ensure the account is appropriate.

How property usage affects tax

Keeping a property register will show how each property is / has been used. This is important because the specific usage dictates whether tax is due, what type of tax should be paid and who has to pay it.

Ownership of a buy to let property can switch between owners.

For buy to let HMOs, the rental business models can vary but, for tax purposes, the type of rental is the same. Owners pay income tax on rental profits and capital gains tax on chargeable gains when the property or a share of the property is disposed of.

Other uses, such as living in the property as a main home, holiday lets, commercial and uncommercial lets attract different tax payments and rules. (An uncommercial let is when a friend or relative lives in a property, generally paying the mortgage and bills but not rent at the same level as a 'standard' tenant would pay.)

A property register tracks these changes of use and owners.

The register should start on the first day of ownership and runs until the property is sold or disposed of, and should contain:

- Date of purchase
- How much was paid or the open market value on the date of first ownership
- Incidental buying costs – like stamp duty and legal fees
- Improvement costs – like the costs of a loft conversion, extension or garage
- Spending on protecting the title – for example, legal costs to establish a fence line
- Incidental sale costs – estate agent charges and legal fees
- Date of disposal and disposal price

A note should also be made of:

- Property use – dates when the property was let or otherwise lived in
- Date of first letting
- Tenancy agreements and rents
- Owners – date they became an owner, percentage share and relationship to other owners

All documents that prove or verify the above information - such as receipts for material improvements, legal bills to protect the title, stamp duty paid and any legal costs - should be kept in the property register.

Apportioning income and expenses to people and properties

Tagging financial records is about setting cost centres. These cost centres fall into two categories: properties and owners.

Tagging income and expenses by property allows the owners to extract the figures they require for their tax returns:

- Capital costs go to the property register and the tax return capital gains tax pages
- Income from tenants, day to day running costs and general business expenses go to the rental accounts and to the tax return property pages

The tagging system also allows investors to see exactly how much each property makes or loses so they can determine their return on investment.

For example, if a property makes a profit of £3,000 and three owners are shown on the property register with owner 1 holding a 50% share and the others each with a 25% share, then the profits are allocated as £1,500 to owner 1 and £750 each to the remaining owners.

Allocating income and expenses to tax years

Rental income and expenses must always be accounted for in the correct tax year. If they run across two tax years, then the cost must be split between them.

For example, buildings insurance costs £180 and runs from January 1 to December 31, crossing two tax years. The cost is apportioned between two tax years:

- January to March (3 months = 3/12 of the expense or £180/12 x 3 = £45)
- April to December (9 months = 9/12 of the expense or £180/12* 9 = £135 or £180 - £45 = £135).

A more precise apportionment would be by days:

- January 1 until April 5 (95 days = 95/365 of the expense, i.e. £180/365 x 95 = £46.85

- April 6 to December 31 (270 days = 270/365 of the expense, i.e. £180/365 x 270 = £133.15)

Pre letting expenses

Pre letting expenses are the costs the landlord has to pay before the date of first letting.

They should be separated out into capital costs and day to day business payments. Capital costs go to the property register, day to day costs go to the rental accounts, as if they were incurred on the first day of letting, so long as:

- Services, such as labour, were incurred up to six months before the date of first letting
- Any goods were charged up to three years before the date of first letting

How long should financial records be kept?

Financial records should be kept for at least six years after the tax year to which they apply has ended. Do not get rid of them, even if you do not make a tax return, as the taxman could ask for them at any point within the six years.

For capital gains tax purposes, the property register should be kept for as long as the owner has an interest in the property and then six years after the property disposal.

Calculating profits or losses

Working out these figures should be straightforward – simply subtract expenses from income. But the key to maximising profits is knowing which costs are allowable business expenses. There is no definitive HMRC list of what can be included in expenses, and things such as business mileage can be complex to work out.

(See 'What landlords can claim against tax' in the next section.)

Take the total income and subtract allowable expenses to give the net rental profit.

Then deduct any allowances, such as 10% for wear and tear - or the renewals allowance if you let a furnished property – and the final figure is the taxable profit or loss.

Dealing with rental losses

Property losses may be carried forward to offset future profits. There is a section on the tax return for this.

If losses are brought forward from a previous tax year, they must be deducted in full to leave the taxable amount. If the losses are more than the profit, the balance can be carried forward to the next tax year with profits.

For example:

> A landlord made a £2,500 loss in 2010 and a £1,500 profit in 2011. The losses brought forward cancel the 2011 profits and £1,000 of losses is carried forward to 2012.
>
> In 2012, the landlord makes a loss of £500, so £1,500 is carried forward to 2013.
>
> In 2013, the landlord makes a £2,000 profit, so the £1,500 loss is deducted, leaving £500 of taxable profits.

Taxpayers cannot select when to use losses; they must be deducted in full against the first available profit.

If the property is under shared ownership, each owner must declare their share of profits or losses. The income and expenses are divided pro rata per ownership share.

VAT

Landlords cannot normally register for value added tax (VAT), as residential rental income is exempt from VAT. This means any VAT incurred cannot be reclaimed.

However, landlords who are VAT registered in their own self employed business may be able to claim back some of the VAT.

Inheritance tax

Many people invest in property because they want an asset to leave to their children. However, depending on your situation and how you have arranged your affairs, property may not be the best investment vehicle for inheritance purposes.

When the owner of a property dies, the value of that property at the time of their death forms part of the estate, so may be liable to inheritance tax.

Inheritance tax can be legitimately reduced. When drawing up a will, landlords can take legal advice on how the estate is best handed down to make maximum use of allowances.

To ensure you mitigate inheritance tax, consult a property tax specialist before you purchase any HMO.

Letting Income / Expenses

Keeping the accounts for a property business is one thing, but landlords must know precisely what makes up income and expenses for the underlying profit and loss calculations, and to ensure they maximise their return on investment. Every expense missed is more tax paid.

Putting income and expenses in the wrong tax years can throw the profit or loss calculations as well, meaning overpaying or underpaying tax for the year. Landlords who are found to have knowingly played the system by altering their figures can be fined by HMRC.

Accurate record keeping is not only important from a tax perspective, but also because it makes administration easier and allows landlords to keep tabs on properties that are failing to perform.

What is rental income?

Rental income is all the money generated by a property business, with the exception of deposits from tenants. (Tenant deposits always remain the property of the tenant, except holding deposits paid to reserve the property while the tenancy agreement is sorted out.) Rental income includes one off payments, so even if a home is let out for only a couple of weeks for an event, such as the Wimbledon tennis championships, the rent must be declared.

Payments for services not normally offered by a landlord - such as cleaning bedrooms, a laundry service or regular meals - will be treated as trading income, not rental income. Separate accounts should be kept for these payments, which are declared as self employment income.

Landlords should note that if they reduce rent in lieu of work done by the tenant, the full rent still counts as income.

Accounting for rent arrears

In accounting terms, rent arrears are bad debts. To set off rent arrears on the accounts as a bad debt, a landlord needs to show HM Revenue and Customs that they have made reasonable efforts to recover the money.

That could involve issuing court action or handing the case to a debt collector.

What are lettings business expenses?

Lettings business expenses are day to day running costs that the landlord pays out to run a property business.

The myth is that there is a list of allowable expenses kept by the taxman. This is not true. As with most tax rules, HM Revenue and Customs manuals cover what can't be claimed, rather than what is allowable.

Keeping precise records of all expenses incurred and using the services of a property tax specialist should mean that allowable business expenses are maximised on your tax return.

What landlords can claim against tax

The most common property business expenses are:

Advertising
Any cost relating to marketing a property. Advertising and letting agents' costs are allowed, but costs of permanent 'to let' signs are considered a capital cost (the costs of selling a house are a capital expense).

Bad and doubtful debts
Rent arrears can only be included in the accounts when the landlord has taken all reasonable steps to recover the debt.

If the debt is later recovered, the landlord should bring in the recovery as a receipt in the year they get the money. A bad debt reserve cannot be carried in the accounts. For example, keeping 5% of their debts 'just to be on the safe side' is not allowed.

Business costs

The expenses relating to administering a property business are allowable – such as telephones, computers, broadband, stationery and other consumables. Books on keeping financial records and software etc are allowable, as are tools for maintenance.

If the items are shared between business and private use, the cost must be apportioned, in the same manner as splitting costs across tax years.

Cost of managing common areas

HMOs have parts of the building that are used in common by the tenants. If so, the landlord can deduct expenditure on the upkeep of the common parts from their rental business profits.

Cost of services

Gardening, cleaning of communal areas, maintenance bills and so on.

Fees for loan finance, etc.

Loan finance charges for a rental business are generally deductible, provided they relate wholly and exclusively to a property let out on a commercial agreement. These include loan fees, commissions, guarantee fees and fees in connection with the security of a loan.

Ground rents and service charges

Home as office

HMRC will allow a £4 a week charge without question. Higher charges need justification and if the letting properties are managed by an agent, any figure above the £4 level is likely to be knocked back.

Insurance

Landlord building and contents insurance is allowable, as are contracts for maintaining boilers.

Interest

Whether charging loan interest to a business is allowable depends not on the source of the money, but on how the money is used.

The loan interest on a mortgage secured against a rental property is deductible. But so is the interest on a landlord's credit card or overdraft if the money was spent on the property business. For instance, the landlord goes to a DIY store and buys £100 of paint and materials to decorate a rental property on a personal credit card. The interest on that £100 is fully deductible as a business expense.

Similarly, the interest on a re mortgage to raise a deposit on a buy to let or HMO is an allowable expense. However, if the mortgage money is spent and then replaced by the landlord from his or her own funds, the interest cannot be claimed.

Owner occupied property

Expenditure on a house, flat or other property that the landlord occupies isn't normally allowed as a deduction in computing rental business profits because it does not satisfy the 'wholly and exclusively' rule.

Where a landlord genuinely runs the rental business from home, they may claim the extra business costs that they incur - such as the cost of extra lighting and heating.

Professional fees

Bills from accountants, lawyers and surveyors are deductible, providing they are not capital costs relating to buying or selling a property

Repairs and renewals

Repairs and maintenance are allowable expenses, but improvements are not. Sometimes the line between the two is thin, for example, replacing a tile on the roof is a repair, as is replacing the entire roof; however, putting in a loft extension is an improvement, which is a capital cost.

Repair costs go into the rental accounts and improvements into the capital register.

Salaries and wages of employees

Salaries and wages that a landlord pays to employees engaged full time or part time in managing the rental business are allowable. This includes any normal pension contributions paid on behalf of employees.

Sometimes an employee is engaged partly to manage the rental business property and partly on private work or other work outside the rental business. Here, a fair and reasonable split has to be made.

A landlord can't deduct anything for the time they spend themselves working in their own rental business. They can deduct any wages or salaries they pay to their spouse, civil partner or other relatives for working in the rental business, provided the amounts paid represent a proper commercial reward for the work done.

Travel

The best way to claim travel expenses is to keep a mileage log and track each journey to the bank, post office, letting agent, etc. and claim at 45p a mile for the travel costs.

Utility bills in void periods

Until April 2015, landlords can also claim for the cost of loft, wall and floor insulation, draught proofing and insulation for hot water systems, up to £1,500 per residential property each year.

** NOT allowed as a business expense:

Business entertaining expenses and gifts

Training.
Seminars, courses and other similar events are considered a cost of investment by HMRC.

Travel not directly associated with running the business.
If you have a letting agent, claiming travel to properties is treated as dubious by HMRC. Landlords also cannot claim the costs of trips to view properties to see if they are suitable to add to a portfolio.

Uncommercial lets, i.e. homes let to family or friends at below market value rents, are tax neutral, so make neither a profit nor a loss. Owners cannot claim any business expenses for these properties, but must pay capital gains tax on disposal.

Capital allowances

A capital allowance is tax relief against investment in plant, machinery, equipment and vehicles for a business, including office equipment, such as computers, cameras and scanners.

The rules on capital allowances are complicated and beyond the scope of this course, so landlords are advised to take professional advice from a property tax specialist, accountant or specialist surveyor.

Wear and tear / renewals allowance

Landlords who rent furnished properties can claim for wear and tear of items such as carpets, beds, televisions and cookers. They may choose whether to claim under the renewals allowance or the wear and tear allowance, but once decided they have to stick with that method.

Renewals allowance allows landlords to claim the cost of furnishings as they are replaced. Any money made in disposing of the old ones (such as selling them online) and the cost of improvements, such as replacing a washing machine with a washer dryer, must be deducted.

Wear and tear allowance allows landlords to claim 10% of the net annual rent each year. This is easy to calculate and keeps things simple. And if landlords have not had to pay out for replacement items in the tax year, they may save more than their actual expenditure. However, if taking a wear and tear allowance, the original cost of the item cannot be claimed.

Capital Gains Tax

Capital gains tax (CGT) is a tax on the gain or profit made when shares of the property or the whole property is sold, given away or otherwise disposed of. There is a tax free allowance and some reliefs are available to reduce the CGT bill.

CGT is an important tax to consider as, over the years, property prices will usually rise. It is important that landlords make the most of the reductions and reliefs available as the amounts at stake can be significant.

The basic concept of CGT is quite straightforward. The final price received for the property (or share of the property), after deducting agent fees and legal costs, is compared to the initial cost of the property, including stamp duty and legal fees. This gives the profit or chargeable gain, and CGT is levied on this amount.

Who pays CGT?

The person that benefits from the property disposal pays the tax - that means anyone receiving cash or any other consideration from the transaction.

CGT reducers

The most important potential deductions and reliefs available are:

- The cost of any improvements can be deducted, but not costs of repairs that have been offset against income tax

- If the landlord has lived in the property as an owner occupier, there are two additional reliefs: lettings relief, where a certain amount of gain per owner can be tax free, and a proportionate private residence relief

- If the property was owned at March 1982, its value at that date is substituted for the original cost of the property

- The set value of any capital gains in a single tax year is tax free per individual, not per property, with tax only charged on gains above that value

- If two properties have been used as residences, it is worth making a principal private residence election on one property.

Calculating CGT

Property owners often worry unnecessarily about capital gains tax, believing the tax due is a lot higher than it really is.

Here is a sample CGT calculation for a buy to let property. The first point to remember is CGT is a backwards calculation that starts with the disposal proceeds:

Disposal proceeds	£285,000
Less	
Purchase price	£150,000
Disposal costs	£6,500
Improvement costs	-
Buying costs	£5,500
	_____
Total costs	(£162,000)
	_____
	_____
Taxable gain	£123,000

Assuming two owners each hold a 50% stake, they divide the gain by 2 to give each a taxable gain of £62,500.

Each owner has a personal annual CGT exemption of £10,900 for 2013-14, which is deducted from the gain by each owner, leaving a chargeable gain of £61,391.

Assuming the couple has no other CGT reliefs or losses to set off against the gain, tax is charged at 18% for basic rate taxpayers (£11,050) and 28% for higher rate taxpayers (£17,189).

NEXT STEPS...

If you have completed this course, worked your way through the various checklists and worksheets and put together some analysis spreadsheets of your own, you should be very well prepared to move forward in your HMO journey.

That's the theory, anyway. In practice, many people find the prospect of actually committing a good deal of time and money to an investment that is entirely under their control a little daunting and that's where a mentor can really help.

Mentoring is by far the most effective way to pass on knowledge and experience and, over the past few years, I have spent a lot of time working with new and existing landlords, helping them start and grow their property portfolios.

Contact my office to discuss your next steps:

Website: nickfox.co.uk
Email: hello@nickfox.co.uk
Office: 01908 930369

Too many people hold back because they think their questions might be silly and that they should already know the answers. But if property investment and/or running your own business is new to you, then there will be hundreds of questions you'll need help finding the answers to and I'm more than happy to share my knowledge and experience with you. As the saying goes, there are no stupid questions

"The only difference between successful people and unsuccessful people is extraordinary determination."
Mary Kay Ash, Entrepreneur

"Some people dream of success, while others wake up and work hard a it."
Sir Winston Churchill

"Your attitude, not your aptitude, will determine your altitude."
Zig Ziglar

Even more...

...from Nick Fox Property Mentoring.

Thank you for taking the time to read our book; we hope you've found it helpful. If you'd like to extend your knowledge, please check out our website, where you'll find a wealth of free information and details of our mentoring packages.

We offer a range of mentoring options to suit all needs, from short intensive taster sessions to more comprehensive packages that will give you a deeper understanding of property investment and the buy to let market, focusing on the rewards and implications of building an HMO portfolio.

Various choices available include:
- Half-day 'HMO Education and Tour'
- One-day 'Intensive HMO Property Mentoring Course'
- Two-day 'Intensive HMO Property Mentoring Course'
- 12 months' full access to and support from Nick Fox and his Power Team

Whichever package you choose, you can be assured that Nick's commitment to your personal property goals are absolute. Nick and his team get a real kick out of watching others grow their property portfolios by helping them implement the most successful methods that have been tried and tested over many years.

As skilled and experienced professionals, we present our mentoring sessions in such a way that they are easy to understand, while enabling highly effective learning. The acute insights and practical methodology on offer will help you to take your property business to the next level and secure financial independence for you and your loved ones.

Check out our website **www.nickfox.co.uk** or call us on **01908 930369** to find out more.

Find us on FACEBOOK Nick Fox Mentor TWITTER @foxytowers
www.nickfox.co.uk EMAIL hello@nickfox.co.uk TEL 01908 930369
NICK FOX PROPERTY MENTORING Suite 150 MK Business Centre
Foxhunter Drive Linford Wood Milton Keynes MK14 6BL

nickfox
property mentoring

Read on...

Collect the set of books by Nick Fox to help you achieve financial freedom through property investment.

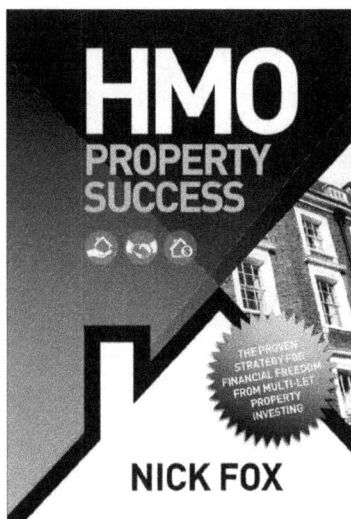

HMO PROPERTY SUCCESS

Do you want a secure financial future that starts sooner, rather than later as you're approaching retirement? By investing in multi-let properties, you can double or even triple the level of rental income generated by single letting, and realise positive cash flow from the start. In this book, multiple business owner and investor, Nick Fox, clearly guides you through the steps to building an HMO portfolio that delivers both on-going income and a tangible pension or lifestyle pot.

ISBN: 978-0-9576516-0-9
RRP: £9.99

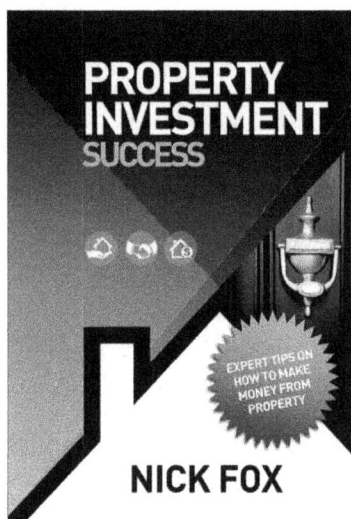

PROPERTY INVESTMENT SUCCESS

How does your financial future look?
If you haven't reviewed your pension provision for a while or aren't completely happy with how your current investments are performing, you should take a closer look at property. In this book, Nick Fox discusses the pros and cons of traditional pensions and makes the case for property as a robust alternative investment vehicle.
He looks at how property can deliver different kinds of returns at different times and shows how you can build a tailored portfolio that perfectly satisfies your own future financial needs.

ISBN: 978-0-9576516-4-7
RRP: £9.99

Available now online at
www.amazon.co.uk & www.nickfox.co.uk
Books, eBook, Kindle & Audio

Find us on **FACEBOOK** Nick Fox Mentor **TWITTER** NickFoxPropertyMentoring
www.nickfox.co.uk **EMAIL** hello@nickfox.co.uk **TEL** 01908 930369
NICK FOX PROPERTY MENTORING Suite 150 MK Business Centre
Foxhunter Drive Linford Wood Milton Keynes MK14 6BL

nickfox
property mentoring

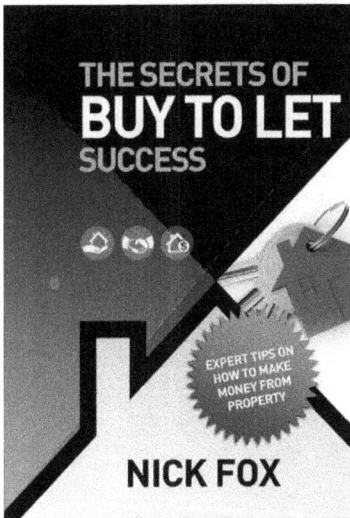

THE SECRETS OF BUY TO LET SUCCESS

Are you looking for a sound investment that can give you both income and growth on your capital, but nervous about the future of the property market? This book will put your mind at rest. In The Secrets of Buy to Let Success, Nick Fox shares his knowledge and expertise about the market, guiding the reader step by step through the basics of building a solid and profitable property business - even through an economic crisis. If you're completely new to property investment, this book is a great place to start.

ISBN: 978-0-9927817-2-9
RRP: £9.99

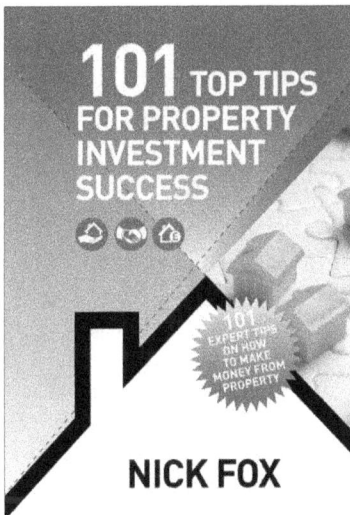

101 TOP TIPS FOR PROPERT INVESTMENT SUCCESS

Whether you're looking to focus purely on HMOs, build a varied portfolio of rental properties, or employ a number of different strategies to make money from property, '101 TOP TIPS' is full of useful information that will help keep you at the top of the property investment business.

Nick Fox has spent the past decade amassing a highly profitable buy to let portfolio and continues to invest in a variety of property projects and business ventures. His tailored mentoring programmes have helped many aspiring investors realise their own potential in the property field.

ISBN: 978-0-9935074-9-6
RRP: £9.99

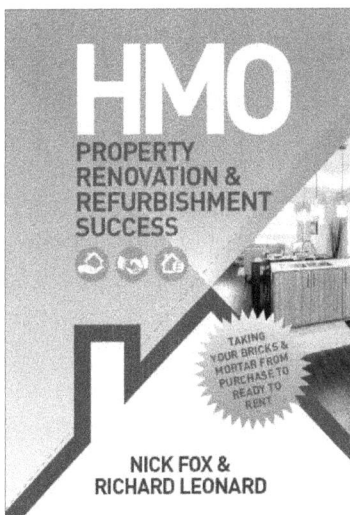

PROPERTY RENNOVATION & REFURBISHMENT SUCCESS

Successful renovation and refurbishment relies on spending the right amount of money in the right way, so are you ready to hone your budgeting, planning and project-management skills? Alongside the deposit, this is where the biggest chunk of your investment funds will be spent. You need to analyse the figures, budget correctly, plan the work in detail and ensure it's carried out properly so that your buy to let performs as you need it to. Not sure how to do that? Then this is the book for you!

ISBN: 978-0-9927817-6-7
RRP: £11.99

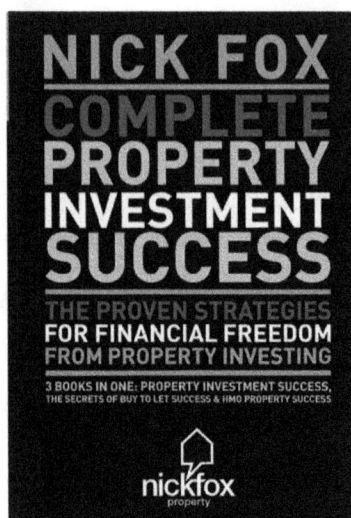

COMPLETE PROPERTY INVESTMENT SUCCESS

This indispensable trilogy takes you through the pros and cons of property as an investment vehicle, looks at the business of buy to let and the different ways you can make money from property, then goes into detail about how to successfully source, refurbish and let out highly cash-positive houses in multiple occupation.

ISBN: 978-0-9927817-0-5
RRP: £26.99

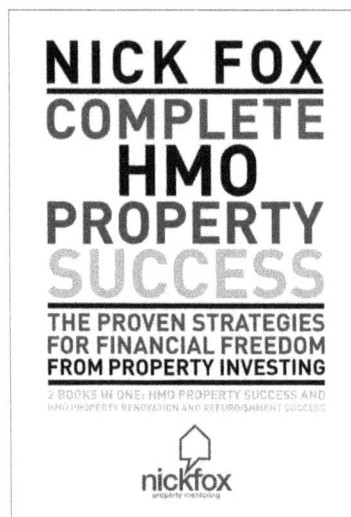

COMPLETE HMO PROPERTY SUCCESS

This HMO 'superbook' is essential reading for anyone who's starting out in property investment and wants to generate income.

It begins by looking at investing in Houses in Multiple Occupation as a business and takes you through how to successfully source, refurbish, let out and manage a highly cash-positive portfolio.

The second part then focuses on the all-important renovation stage. It details how to budget, plan your works, manage your project and carry out the refurbishment in such a way that your HMO performs as you need it to and you get the returns you're looking for.

A prolific and highly successful investor, Nick's personal portfolio extends to more than 200 properties, both shared accommodation and single household lets – and he also has interests in several development projects around the UK.

ISBN: 978-0-9935074-0-3 | RRP: £19.99

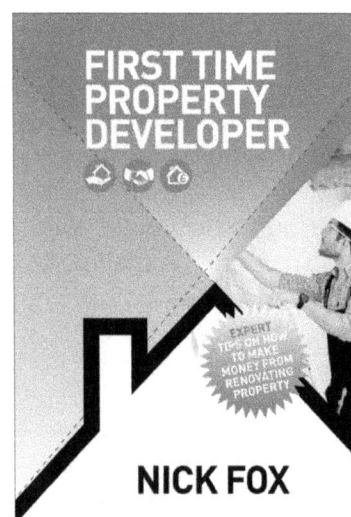

FIRST TIME PROPERTY DEVELOPER

Interested in developing property for profit ? Don't know where to start? Let experienced property expert, Nick Fox, lead you through the process. Nick will show you how to find the property, add genuine value to it by developing and refurbishing and then explain how to sell on for profit or rent out for income.

ISBN: 978-0-9576516-4-7
RRP: £9.99

www.nickfox.co.uk

Write a review and get free stuff!

If you've enjoyed what you've read, why not tell other people and bag yourself some free stuff in the process?

Simply write a review of this compilation — or any of the other books in the 'SUCCESS' series and publicise it via:

- Amazon
- iTunes
- Facebook
- Twitter
- Your blog

... or any other online or offline publications.

Then email an image or link to us at hello@nickfox.co.uk.

We'll thank you via Twitter and you'll get back some exclusive property investment tools and samples of our latest materials to help you stay focused and up to date in your investment journey.

Thanks in advance and we hope to hear from you soon!

Testimonials

This is just some of the positive feedback I've received from happy mentoring clients over the past few years:

"I met Nick a number of years ago and was immediately struck by his deep knowledge and experience in the field of property investing. No problem is ever too great a challenge for Nick - his creative entrepreneur spirit is a joy to behold. He is both dynamic and detailed, great fun to work with and quite truly inspirational. He is now my business partner and good friend."
Richard Leonard

"Nick and his team are the real deal. Their knowledge and help in moving my investment project forward has been invaluable. Without their expertise I would not have been able to reach my personal property goals or milestones."
Richard Felton, UK

"Great book, great guy and great results for me after I read 'HMO Property Success'. I've now replaced my job with passive income from HMO properties. Thanks, Nick!"
C.Clark, Bedford

"Nick is a very experienced property professional. His practical advice on setting goals, the pros and cons of this type of investment and how to minimise risks and properly manage a growing portfolio are essential in what can be a very complex investment. Nick's mentoring is not a get-rich-quick formula but a clear and concise way of demonstrating how a solid property investment strategy can be put into action. And the results are well worth it."
D.Wright, Aberdeen

"I have spent money in the past on various property courses, where you are taught in a group in a classroom, and those have not really helped me. This one-to-one mentoring with Nick was brilliant, as I was actually seeing his business and properties, meeting tenants, getting lots of advice and seeing what worked well and what didn't in a live situation. I have booked another two days with Nick in my home city next week, to look at various properties and hopefully start my journey as a full-time property investor, and I cannot wait! I highly recommend this type of mentoring!"
James Robinson, Hull

"Both Sarah and I cannot express how much help Nick has been to our property business over the last two years. His support and knowledge have been invaluable.

We would thoroughly recommend his mentoring to any budding investor."
Stuart Lewis, Northampton

"Thank you so much for your patience, professionalism and general understanding during our three-day mentoring programme. The visit to see how your office and HMO business runs was incredible and so, so helpful. Without it we would have been at a complete loss. With your guidance and help we have now purchased our first HMO property and look forward to keeping in touch to show you our profitable progress!"
Rebecca Santay-Jones, Harrow

"I first met Nick in the autumn of 2012 when I was looking for someone to guide me through my first HMO purchase. Nick's mentoring was invaluable and gave me such a good grounding - not just in HMOs, but in how to run a successful property business - that I have been able to move forward with real confidence as my business has grown. Even now, if there is something I am uncertain of, or I just want to bounce an idea around, I'm very grateful to have Nick in my corner. He has such wide-ranging experience in the industry and I value his opinion greatly. The income my portfolio already provides gives me the option of going part-time in my day job and in the coming months, as I grow the business further, I fully intend to become a full-time property investor and landlord."
Andy Potter, Fareham

"Today's experience has been brilliant – it really opened up my eyes up to the world of HMOs and made me see properties in a different light, in terms of understanding just how much potential each one has. Your experience has accelerated my learning and shown me how important it is to have the right mindset when getting into this area of property investing.

As a kinaesthetic learner, I really enjoyed the hands-on experience of going from property to property and getting a flavour of how you see and do things. Your openness and honesty is what I appreciated the most and has reaffirmed to me that I have made the right choice. Looking forward to getting that first property!"
Gabriel F, Enfield

"Nick has clearly got a huge amount of knowledge in his field, and having his support and experience has given me the increased confidence to make my first steps into investing."
Craig Smith, Edinburgh